THE ORVIS BOOK
OF
UPLAND BIRD
SHOOTING

THE ORVIS BOOK

OF

UPLAND BIRD

SHOOTING

by

GEOFFREY NORMAN

Illustrated by

RICHARD HARRINGTON

Nick Lyons Books

Winchester Press

An Imprint of New Century Publishers, Inc.

FOR GEORGE ROBIN SWIFT, JR.
Who taught me how

Published and distributed by
WINCHESTER PRESS
New Century Publishers
220 Old New Brunswick Road
Piscataway, New Jersey 08854

Produced by
NICK LYONS BOOKS
31 West 21st Street
New York, New York 10010

PRINTED IN THE UNITED STATES OF AMERICA
10 9 8 7 6 5 4 3 2 1

LIBRARY OF CONGRESS CATALOGING-IN-PUBLICATION DATA

Norman, Geoffrey.
The Orvis book of upland bird shooting.

"Nick Lyons books."
1. Upland game bird shooting. I. Title.
SK323.N67 1985   799.2'42   85–17780
ISBN 0–8329–0412–0

Contents

Contents

Preface

You hunt birds in the fall. It is the harvest season and that lends an air of seriousness, almost gravity, to the sport. The woods and the fields have bloomed and borne their fruit and now they are on the verge of returning to that dormant, near barren state for another season, with everything turning cold and grey as the bare earth.

But for a short time, not more than a few weeks, there will be a feeling of abundance to almost everything. Seeds, nuts, and fruit will everywhere be ripe and ready to fall or to rot on the ground. The air will be full of birds making their way to winter grounds. At night, on the big harvest moon, you can stand outside and watch the wavering lines of geese against the dim yellow sky. Salmon and brown trout will be spawning. Young deer, the summer's fawn, will be losing their spots and leaving their mothers.

The evening will arrive earlier and turn cooler and you will feel the coming of the first killing frost. The morning chill will cut a little deeper each day and you will begin burning the firewood you laid in over the summer and picking the last tender vegetables from the garden.

There is something undeniably melancholy about this time of year but, if you are a bird hunter, you will love it like no other.

There will be those days when a big high-pressure area covers your part of the country and temperatures the night before have dropped to near freezing as the land gives up its accumulated warmth through a cloudless sky. There may be a thin coating of white frost on the ground for the first hour after the sun comes up. It will be a while before the birds begin actively feeding.

You will notice the cold yourself when you first start out but then the unconsciously pleasurable effort of walking will begin to move your blood and bring it to the surface and you will be as warm as you need to be, even though you might still be able to see your own breath. The stiffness of the night will leave you quickly and you will feel fluid and supple, ready to walk all day behind your dog who, for his part, is more than ready to run and hunt all day.

The signs of the season will be all around you: the changing leaves, the birds and animals feeding with that urgency that comes with this time of year; the sound, perhaps, of geese passing high overhead, honking to one another across their graceful formations.

Somewhere as you walk, taking in all this perishable beauty, the dog will stiffen to point ahead of you. You will feel your heart as you walk up to him. Then the bird—or birds—will come up and you will shoot. The bird falls and the dog retrieves. You hold your kill. It is still warm, beaded here and there with drops of blood. The dark functional hues of its feathers are beautiful no matter what kind of game bird it is, whether it is a cock or a hen. You admire the bird for a while. It rests limply in your hand.

What you feel now is neither remorse nor regret. Not specifically a sadness, either. There is a time to everything, the book says, and this is the time of the harvest. A time when many things die. It is the time when we are most keenly aware of mortality—our own and that of other living things around us. You can almost smell mortality on the air in the woodsmoke and the scent of burning leaves. See and taste it in the ripe bursting fruit and grain. And you can apprehend it in the slight weight of the bird that you have just killed. So what you feel is loftier than mere sadness. Keener. It is a kind of satisfying melancholy. The sort of feeling poets manage so effortlessly but that comes with more difficulty to the rest of us.

So bird hunting is serious business—though certainly not grim. It is sport after all. The best sport in the world for many of us. The best thing you can do at the best time of the year.

There is no way a book can make it appreciably better. But

anything is improved, even if only slightly, when you use the right tools and the best techniques. And since the season for hunting birds is so lamentably short, there is often nothing to do for the longing you feel for that time of year except to read about bird hunting and then let your imagination wander off to better days, when you could be out under a wide autumn sky, following a dog that is making game.

So for that reason, here is another book about hunting upland game birds. May it be instructive if not exhaustive. Evocative if not thoroughly expert. And may it at least give the occasional reader a clearer window onto that thing that we do in the dwindling days of the year, when everything is ripe and ready to fall.

1

Correct Conduct

The successful bird hunter must be knowledgeable about many things but in the end it comes down to this: he must know his birds, his dogs, and his guns. He cannot really become an accomplished bird hunter if he is ignorant of any of these. He will not be successful, he will not enjoy himself, and, in the bargain, he may be dangerous.

So of the three primary subjects, it is probably best to begin with guns. Without guns, it would not be a hunt. (Before there were guns with which to hunt, European noblemen used dogs to point, and falcons to kill, their birds.) And the presence of the gun on the hunt is enough to make it serious business. You should learn to handle guns before you even try to learn about handling dogs or shooting birds.

While learning to handle guns is serious business, it is anything but onerous. Anyone who was raised around guns remembers the first time his father took him out to shoot and remembers it keenly as one of those moments in childhood when the door to a whole new world suddenly opened wide. Your first gun is something you remember in the same vivid fashion. Learning about guns and learning to shoot are among the very best memories for whole generations of men. For them, it was the stuff of ritual, a kind of rite of passage, and they took it very seriously indeed. If they had not, their fathers would have taken their guns away and they might never have learned.

Of course, the country has become urbanized and not many boys these days grow up learning about guns. Many fathers, in fact, are unable to teach a boy who wants to learn. That tradition has shrunk.

But you can still learn to shoot, even if you are grown and have never in your life held a gun in your hands. In a way, this is an improvement over the old way. It lacks the romance of fathers passing on wisdom to their sons but it probably turns out better shooters. In the old days, many fathers passed on their bad habits to their sons. Thousands of men who had learned first to shoot a rifle, then made the transition to a shotgun without changing technique at all, spent a lifetime shooting a shotgun improperly and poorly. They treated the shotgun as a rifle that fired a lot of bullets and had a shorter range. Treated it, that is, as a kind of inferior rifle.

Today, you can go to school to learn how to shoot a shotgun. It can almost be considered a form of continuing adult education. You are taking course work that, for one reason or another, you missed earlier. The instructors at these schools can make you into an adequate shooter in two or three days or, if you already are adequate, they might be able to make you into a good shooter. If you are lucky, they can correct the mistakes that you have been making, out of habit, all your life. The techniques they use were developed over the years in England where the shotgun is the primary sporting weapon, no doubt because the population density makes it unsafe to hunt much with a rifle and because there isn't the game for it. But the British are famous for their shotguns and they have studied the art of shooting them with the same earnestness that they have applied to the art of making them.

You may not come away from a profit-making shooting school with the same deep fund of memory that learning from your father would have given you, but you might actually come out a better shot.

No matter how you learn, you should begin with a few fundamentals. And the most fundamental of all fundamentals, when it comes to shooting, is safety.

———•———

Bird hunters carry loaded guns in the field. They hunt with a partner and, sometimes, with several other people. They hunt near farms and in other populated rural areas. The potential for an accident is always there. So the hunter must be conscious, at all times, of the fact that he is carrying a gun. And he must always treat that gun as if it were loaded. This is, and always has been, the first great rule of gun safety. *Treat every gun as though it were loaded.* It has been said countless times by countless fathers and range instructors, and it still has not been said enough.

Now, even though you should treat every gun, at all times, as though it were loaded, there are times when it absolutely should not be. Do not, for instance, ride in a car with a loaded gun. It is against the law in many jurisdictions. It is dangerous everywhere.

If you are hunting off horseback or out of a vehicle, wait until you are on the ground to load up.

Unload, or break your gun at the breech, when you hand it to another hunter. And never, of course, point the muzzle at him when you do it—even if you *know* the gun is unloaded.

Carry the gun with the muzzle pointed either to heaven or to earth. When you think about which way to point it, think about your partner. If he is behind you, point the muzzle ahead and down. If he is in front of you, carry the gun over your shoulder, with the muzzle pointed up.

Keep the safety on until you are ready to shoot. This does not mean that you should flick the safety off as soon as you see the dog go on point and then walk up to him with your gun ready to shoot as soon as you touch the trigger. Flicking the safety from "on" to "off" should be part of what you do when you mount the gun to shoot. It is one of the last things you do before you touch the trigger and, after you have done it enough, you won't even be aware that you are doing it. Then, once you have made your shot, check automatically to make sure that you have returned the safety to the "on" position. Check it, too, from time to time between shots. And do not

rely on the safety. Some of them are not mechanically sound and many that are have a way of being in the "off" position even when a shooter is sure that they are "on." The safety is important but it does not relieve you of the duty to follow the first rule of gun safety. Do not carelessly point your gun muzzle at your partner or your dog thinking that it is all right because the safety is "on."

Be sure of your shells. Many hunters own guns of different bores and it is possible to drop, say, a twenty-eight-gauge shell into the chamber of a twenty-gauge gun. Later you check the breech, decide you have forgotten to load, and drop in a shell of the correct size. When you fire that barrel, the twenty-eight-gauge shell is still in there, and the gun blows up. A barrel obstruction can be lethal and it will certainly ruin a shotgun. Make sure you are carrying shells only for the gun you are shooting on that hunt.

Be sure of your target. Rifle hunters who shoot someone accidentally almost always violate this rule. They see movement and they shoot, thinking that what they see is a deer, or might be a deer, when in fact it is another hunter. A good bird hunter should be shooting at flying birds and it is hard to mistake a man for a flying bird. But just the same, keep in mind that you should always be absolutely sure of your target before you pull the trigger. It can be an important factor for the bird hunter when he is shooting pheasant. If only cocks are legal game, he cannot shoot on the flush but must wait until he hears the unmistakable squawk or sees the brilliant green head before he pulls the trigger. Also, on close-holding birds, like woodcock, it is possible to catch the dog with part of the shot pattern if you shoot too quickly, without making sure of your target. So with any kind of game, with any kind of gun, it is important to be sure of what you are shooting at. This is the second great law of gun safety. *Treat every gun as if it were loaded and armed, and always be sure of what you are shooting at*.

Follow these two rules without fail, and you will not be involved in one of those sad, stupid, preventable hunting accidents that make such doleful reading in the newspapers.

One final note on safety. A bird hunter needs to pay attention to where his partner is. In heavy cover, which is where grouse hunters spend most of their time, you can be within a few yards of someone and not see him at all. If the bird flushes between you, and you both shoot, you could wind up picking shot out of each other's hides. Or, if you are walking abreast and get out of perfect alignment, when a bird flushes and one hunter swings on it, he may draw the muzzle across his partner and shoot at just the wrong moment.

Check on your partner frequently. If you are in thick cover, talk to each other to make sure you know your relative locations. And wear some kind of hunter-visible clothing. An orange hat or vest can save you a lot of fumbling and uncertainty . . . or worse.

There is no way courtesy and etiquette could be as important to bird hunting as safety is. But it says an awful lot about the sport that they are *almost* as important. You should pass up a safe shot now and then—for instance when the muzzle of your gun is close enough to your partner's head that the noise will give him a headache. You should pass up shots at birds that flush across your partner's line of fire even if he is slow to mount unless you have been hunting together long enough that you can be sure he wants you to take a shot because he has something in his eye or has forgotten to load his gun.

You shouldn't give commands to another man's dog and you certainly shouldn't say anything about the dog that isn't good. The owner of a dog has either worked hard or paid good money to train the dog to do his bidding. Commands from someone other than his master will merely confuse him and criticism will probably infuriate his master, even if he says all sorts of things about the dog that are worse. This is his prerogative.

You shouldn't shoot anything over another man's dog except game the dog has been broken to hunt. If a rabbit gets up in front of you, pass it up unless the owner of the dog has told you it is all right to shoot rabbits.

Move at the pace of the slowest hunter.

Don't make excuses.

Don't hog game.

Try to be a good companion as well as a good hunter. Bird hunting is as companionable as deer hunting is solitary. A few hunters prefer to go out alone but most go with at least one partner. Regular, long-term partnerships are common and take on a personality that is separate from the personality of either individual. It can be something like a durable marriage, that way. You hear of bird-hunting partnerships that have lasted from boyhood through early twenties and on until both men were nearly old. And then, when one of them dies, the other gives up bird hunting entirely.

On the other hand, you also hear of bird-hunting partnerships that have broken up over unsafe gun handling or game hogging or because someone disparaged a dog that didn't belong to him. What it comes down to is—as the man who taught me used to say—if you are going to be a bird hunter, first you have to learn how to act right. A great day in the field is, by definition, one where everyone acts right. The birds hold, the dogs find and point them, and the hunters shoot and behave correctly.

Then, it is all sublime.

2

First
Shots

Learning to shoot a shotgun takes time. Learning anything takes time. If it doesn't take time, then it isn't learning when you acquire a new skill. It's revelation. Most people who have been around long enough to know will tell you that there never has been a good shot who got there through grace.

You will see some who hope to get there that way. They go out into the woods and fields time after time hoping to hit what they shoot at, more or less convinced that they won't, but hoping, perhaps, that on this day the lightning will strike. It never does. Shooters like that may get lucky now and again but they don't put two good days together and they never feel comfortable about shooting.

That's because they never took the trouble to learn to shoot.

Learning anything is generally a matter of getting familiar with some very fundamental theory—most aviators are not engineers but almost all of them understand Bernouli's Theorem, which is the scientific explanation for why airplanes fly. If you want to shoot a shotgun properly, it helps to know how it is a shotgun delivers its payload. You do not have to understand how steel alloys differ from one another or vector theory. But you should be able to formulate an analogy and imagine a picture of how everything works when you pull the trigger and, out there forty yards, a bird crumples.

The best illustration that I ever heard was this: imagine the shotgun as a garden hose. No single projectile comes out of it—rather, a string of many pellets, like so many drops of water. The image of a garden hose tracking a moving target will help you considerably in understanding leads, shot strings, and patterns—all of which you will need to understand in order to shoot truly well.

When you touch the trigger of a shotgun and explode the powder in a shell, pellets leave the muzzle in a column. It has both width and depth. The width tends to expand as the column of shot travels farther from the barrel. It also stretches out some. When you fire at a stationary piece of paper, what you see is the pattern of shot at whatever range you fired from. You can draw a circle around that portion of the pattern where the holes are so close together that anything inside it would surely be killed—where, generally speaking, about 80 percent of the pellets are. If you swing on a moving target, the pattern will not be the same. It will stretch out and gain some length from the stringing effect. Once you are able to visualize the effects of string and pattern, you will have a better understanding of what happens downrange, when you raise and fire at a fast-flying bird.

After this modicum of theory, the next stage in the learning process is mastering technique. This is where you learn the form and the movements and, if you are impatient, you will practically go blind with boredom. It is also where you will wonder to yourself if this or that posture is really so important since you can remember seeing someone who stood with a completely different stance and put the fine grind on clay birds down at the old Valley Skeet Club.

There is no absolutely correct posture or stance for shooting a shotgun. Shooters will vary one to another, just as golfers address the ball differently and baseball hitters step into the box differently. Pete Rose got a lot of hits with a stance that was hardly classic and Arnold Palmer changed the game of golf with a swing that was much too quick and jerky to be called a thing of beauty. Likewise, there are some fine gunners who do not mount the gun classically.

Still, you should learn what is ideal and then start compromising to suit your own needs. Think the way Plato did. There is the world of pure form out there and, then, in the here and now there are numerous imperfect approximations. Learn the correct technique and then adjust toward your own style. It never helped anyone to start out using bad technique. Furthermore, learning correct technique is a way of learning consistency. Nothing will hurt a shooter more than to position his head and body differently on every shot. Learning the classic techniques (which we shall discuss presently) is a way to make you shoot every shot the same way and that is better than half the battle.

Finally, once you have sampled the theory and learned about technique, you must practice to learn. Learning takes time because it is repetitive. To become a good shot, you must shoot, and shoot a lot. One of the strongest recommendations for shooting schools is that the student gets to shoot a lot of shotgun shells. Hundreds in a couple of days. Shooting a gun becomes instinctive through sheer brute repetition and you will not be a good shooter until you are an instinctive shooter.

You can begin practicing simply by swinging a gun through an arc, imagining as you do it that you are tracking a bird. Snap off an imaginary shot and watch what happens to the gun barrel. If it stops, you have work to do.

Before you actually begin shooting, or even dry firing, test to see which eye is dominant. For most right handers, the right eye will be dominant; with left handers, the reverse will be true. For a few shooters, however, the dominant eye will be opposite the dominant hand. Check by forming a circle with the thumbs and fingers of your hands. Extend your arms fully and sight on an object through this circle with both eyes open. Close the eye opposite the hand you use. The object will not move if the open eye is your dominant eye.

If it should turn out that you are right handed, say, but have a dominant left eye, then you will have to shoot a shotgun with your left eye closed. It isn't fatal. It will cost you some depth perception but you can learn to compensate. If your right eye is dominant and you shoot from the right shoulder, then keep both eyes open when you shoot.

Dry-firing exercise is good drill for keeping the gun moving through the shot and for keeping your head over the gun correctly and your left hand doing what it should be doing, but it can get old pretty fast. Your concentration will go, your mind will wander and, then, the exercise is pointless.

It's more fun to be shooting something. One answer is the BB gun. You can use it in a back yard or some similar safe place without making a lot of noise or spending a lot of money or, if you are a new shooter or a small shooter, having to worry about the gun's recoil.

Since the idea behind shooting a shotgun is to shoot what you point at and not what you aim at, it is important to remove the sights from the BB gun before you begin practicing. If you get in the habit of aiming, your practice will probably make you a worse shot than if you hadn't practiced at all.

Start with targets on the ground. Take a proper stance, turned about a 45-degree angle away from your target, with your shooting shoulder away from the target. Look at the target and on a three count, without taking your eyes off the target, bring the gun smoothly to your shoulder, throwing your left hand as far out in front of you as it is possible to extend it comfortably. Imagine that you are pointing at the target with your left hand. If the gun has a safety that allows it, take the safety off as you are mounting the gun. Keep your eyes on the target. Do not close one eye—keep them both open.

When the gun is firmly mounted, your head will go over the barrel. There is as much controversy over whether the head should be high or low over the barrel as there is among astronomers over whether or not the universe had a beginning or has always been. I can't settle either dispute and, at some point, both shooters and physicists have to weigh the evidence and make a decision. You pays your money and you makes your choice, as the man once said. Some good shooters sight low along the barrel and others keep their heads nearly erect when they mount and shoot the gun. One thing can be safely said: nobody does it one way on one shot and the other on the next.

Using your left hand, point the barrel of the gun at what you are looking at. You either will or will not see the barrel, depending on whether or not you believe the universe had a beginning or has always been. Some good shooters insist they always see the barrel and some say they never do. In any event, *point. Do not aim.* And shoot.

Do this for a few minutes and you will be surprised at how close you come to your target and, indeed, how often you hit it. For one thing, since you see the BB in flight, you can make corrections from shot to shot. It won't be long before you will be confident that you can hit what you point at.

Now go to moving targets. Try a Frisbee that is thrown across your line of fire in the vertical. That will give you a six or eight-inch circle, traveling fairly slowly, to shoot at. Probably you will neglect to move your gun all the way through the flight of the Frisbee and stop to shoot. You will miss, shooting behind your target. Then, to compensate, you will push the barrel a good ways out ahead of the target, stop it, and then shoot. You will miss this way, too—usually shooting ahead but sometimes behind. Finally, if you keep working, you will swing with the flight of your target, letting your left hand push the barrel vigorously through its arc, and shoot as the barrel catches the target and continues to move with it and then ahead of it. And you will start to hit fairly regularly given the uncertain ballistics of the ammunition you are using.

Now you are ready to move up to a real shotgun.

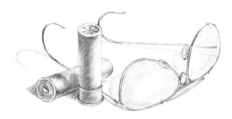

3

Shooting
School

I learned to shoot the old-fashioned way. I wouldn't trade it for anything: days in the field when I was still too young to shave, walking with my father or my favorite uncle, watching the dogs and trying to keep up a grown man's end of the conversation.

When I needed practice shooting, there were dove hunts where a boy could shoot three or four boxes of shells through an old Fox side-by-side sixteen-gauge and never quite get his limit. Or, better, go down to the sawmill with all the shells that were old enough to be suspect and set up outside one of the storage sheds while somebody went inside and pitched a stone up into the rafters.

Then, out came the pigeons.

They had to be shot. They messed up the wood something terrible, according to my uncle who owned the sawmill and had enough trouble without having to hire extra men to clean the pigeon mess off stacked two-by-fours. So I was deputized to shoot them and I did it until my arm got sore. It was great practice and I suppose it provided a service of a sort. Some of the mill hands even ate the pigeons.

Anyway, that is how I learned to shoot, and by the time I was grown I could go on any hunt I was lucky enough to be invited on without worrying about embarrassing myself. That didn't mean I could go hoping to be top gun. Only that I was fairly sure that I could hold my own. It always worked out.

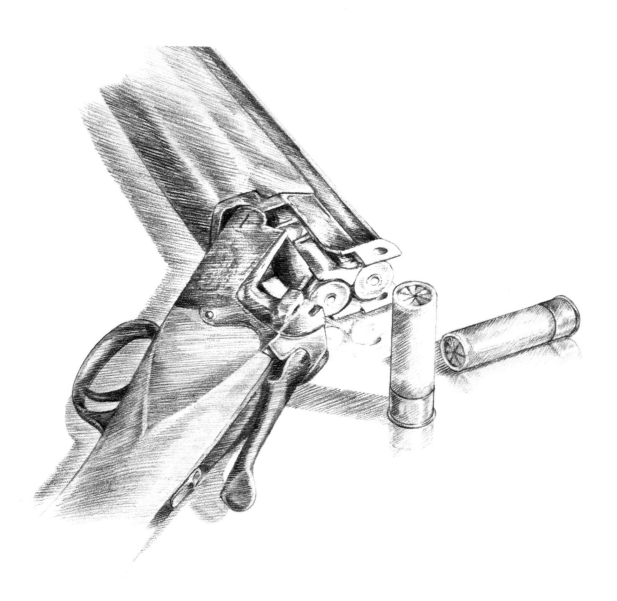

I never even thought about going to a shooting school.

Then I married a woman who wanted to shoot—with me—but had never had any real experience with guns. I knew she could shoot once she'd had some instruction since she is a superb athlete. I knew that because many people who'd been humbled by her on a tennis court had told me so. And I had seen her learn how to fly fish competently in the space of a single season in spite of the fact that she had for a teacher none other than . . . me. And nobody in this world would learn from me unless they could not possibly get out of it, which my wife couldn't.

But even I knew that it probably wouldn't be a good idea for me to try to teach her to shoot. Because some kinds of mistakes in shooting can have consequences far more serious than would follow even the worst mistake in fly casting, a shooting instructor needs to exercise considerable—and even forceful—authority over his students. He needs to be able to raise his voice without worrying about hurting feelings. He can't be a diplomat in matters of gun safety. I try to treat my wife with courtesy and wasn't sure that was the best approach when teaching someone to shoot. I'd been a range instructor briefly in the service and my methods had relied on anything but courtesy.

And then . . . I wasn't really sure I knew enough to teach anybody anything about shooting a shotgun, even though I had fired a lot of shells at a lot of birds since the first time I went out with my father and a friend and a pointer bitch named Dixie, me carrying an old single-shot four-ten that I had actually managed to get up quickly enough to kill one bird on the first covey rise of the day. It had been a long time, and a lot of flushes before I brought down my second bird. Since then, I had killed enough, as I say, to feel confident about my shooting.

But I couldn't, for love or money, say how or what I did. I wasn't sure whether I shot with my eyes open, like most experts said you should (unless you had an eye-dominance problem) or closed one eye and sighted down the barrel which, I knew from reading the sporting magazines, was no good. I wasn't sure whether I led a crossing bobwhite by a bird length or two or merely covered the bird with the gun barrel and shot as I was swinging through him . . . the way people writing in the sporting magazines said it should be done. Some of them, anyway. Others insisted on leads. I *knew* that I led ducks at long range but other birds I simply shot without really knowing how.

I didn't know where my face was, relative to the gun stock, when I shot. I didn't know where my left hand was on the forestock. I didn't know how I mounted the gun, or what combination of factors led to the decision to touch the trigger *right now*, and shoot.

I just went out and did it, the way I learned to do it on a lot of covey rises when I was a kid and on dove fields and on those hapless sawmill pigeons. Which was not a lot of help to anyone other than me.

But we were living near Manchester, Vermont, when my wife decided she wanted to learn how to shoot birds. And Manchester is the headquarters of the Orvis Company. We knew the company had a shooting school and we'd heard good things about it from a couple of people who had attended. So my wife signed up. I was relieved.

She left the school, after three days, fully confident and ready for the bird season that was still a week or two off. I was skeptical but didn't say so. I didn't see how anybody could teach in three days what it had taken me half my youth and a good part of my adulthood to learn, and learn imperfectly, at that.

Bird season came and . . . well, you know the rest. My wife shot well, so well that I had to concede that the school had done a better job in a few days than my intuitive, trial and error, method had accomplished in several years. I was delighted, of course, and curious as well. How, I wondered, had they done it.

About a year later, a few weeks before the opening of bird season, I had a chance to find out. Leigh Perkins, the owner of Orvis, invited me to give the school a try. I knew Perkins slightly and he knew that I was a writer. I expect that, in addition to being a very generous

man, Perkins hoped that I might find something in the school experience to write about. To sweeten the offer, he invited my wife
back for a little post-graduate work.

Now, this time I was genuinely skeptical and even a little wor-
ried. I fancied myself as analogous to a golfer who has learned to play
by caddying and knocking the hell out of balls out on the driving
range but who has never had a lesson. Through hard work and will
power, he has become a very unorthodox low-handicap player. What
he does may not be pretty but it works for him. Should he try to
change it, attempt to groove his swing to look the way a golf swing
should, then he will lose it all. In short, I thought I was too good to
be taught and that the only thing a school might do for my shooting
would be to make it worse.

But I went anyway. Partly because my wife was convinced I
should and partly because I was curious.

So one fine fall morning—it was early September and the leaves
were just moving into their brief and dramatic and dazzling period
of color—we signed in at the little building out back that was the
home of the Orvis schools. We knew the instructors and they wel-
comed us. Then we met the other students. A half dozen of them,
perhaps. There were not many more students than instructors. We
would be getting plenty of individual instruction. Whether that was
good or bad, I couldn't yet be sure.

First, the head of the school introduced himself and gave us a
quick introduction to the school and its rules. The safety precautions
were sound and sensible. Only instructors were allowed to load guns.
All guns were to be broken when the shooter was not actually on the
firing line. No safeties were to be pushed into the "off" position until
the gun was being mounted. All guns were to be treated as though
they were loaded at all times. Shooters at a station who were waiting
to shoot had to leave their guns racked until called to the firing line.

This was all good, sensible stuff and I was glad to hear it.

Next, we saw a movie. This particular film was not more than
thirty minutes long. It was made by the Holland and Holland Com-

pany in England, which runs a famous shooting school of its own. At that school they teach what is known as the Churchill Method, which is named for its founder (who is not *the* Churchill but another one, named Robert) who is the founder of the "no forward allowance" school of shotgunning.

In the film, a stout and very serious Englishman wearing plus fours walks down a path carrying a fine double gun and powdering every clay pigeon that comes sailing out of several concealed positions along the way. He is very formal, precise, and lethal about all of it. And comic in the way English are, especially at the moment when they are taking themselves most seriously. This is the orthodox way of shooting winged game, goes the buried message of this film; heretics will miss shots and bring scorn down upon the heads of themselves and their descendants. I wanted to laugh, except . . . that limey could sure as hell shoot.

So I tried hard to pay attention during the film and the discussion that followed. Later, I even got hold of the book that describes the Churchill Method in detail and studied it. The book is quite technical and I'm not sure that I understood it all. But after seeing the movie, listening to the instructors explain it, and reading the book, I think I have a fair understanding of the Churchill Method. And though I was too far along in my own ways to go over to it completely, I was able to use all of the theory and some of the practice in my own shooting.

There is no way to put it all in a paragraph or two. There is an entire book devoted to the subject, after all. But it is fair, I think, to say that there are some essential components of the Churchill Method. One of the most important is that the shooter does not aim the gun. His eyes are on the target. Always.

Next, since you do not aim the gun, you must do something to make it shoot where you want it to shoot. This means you point. And, if right handed, you point with your left hand. Which means that your left hand must be extended as far out along the forestock, and even the barrel, of the gun as it will go. As your left hand points at the target, which your eyes are already locked onto, the barrel will necessarily also be pointed at it. Simple enough.

Then, you do not try to calculate a lead or shoot to a spot or any of that. What you do is keep your eyes on the target, keep your left hand pointed at it, and move with the flight of the target. When you are moving with it and catch up with it, you fire. But you do not stop looking at the target or pointing at it with your left hand. You touch the trigger, the gun fires, and the bird falls. Quite simple, don't you see.

Now it does sound almost too good to be true. And if you know anything about ballistics, it sounds impossible. But you cannot deny the results you see in the Holland and Holland movie. Or that you will see in your own shooting if you trust the instructors and Mr. Churchill and simply point and shoot, keeping your eye on the target all the way.

I didn't believe, not entirely anyway, when we left and drove off to the shooting stations about three miles away. I'd seen too many demonstrations of why you must shoot in front of a moving target. I'd set up some of those demonstrations myself. Shoot straight at a moving target and in the time, though brief, that the bullet or shot string is in flight, the target will have moved from the place where it was when you aimed and fired. You will hit that place . . . but not the target. It isn't even very complicated physics. So how could Mr. Churchill say "no forward allowance"? And, more to the point, how could that plump little fellow in the plus fours powder those clay birds if he wasn't leading them?

To find out, I made up my mind to try to do it the Churchill way. On the first of the several stations, I was shooting a fairly easy crossing shot. The bird would leave from either my left or right and sail out across in front of me at a relatively shallow angle. It is close to the center station shot in a round of skeet. Not a furiously tough shot, but one where I'd always thought you would need to apply a couple of feet of lead.

The instructor worked the controls to the throwing machine and

I missed the first few shots. I was trying to jump all over the bird and shoot almost before it was out of the machine.

"Relax," the instructor said.

"Right."

"Keep the head up. Eyes on the bird. Move the left hand out as far as it will go and point it at the bird. Move the gun and shoot when you catch up with the bird. Follow through."

"Right."

Thwang.

Bam.

Miss.

"You stopped. Shot behind it. You've got to follow through. And keep the head and eyes up. Don't watch the gun barrel, watch the target."

"Right."

Thwang.

Bam.

Miss.

"Too quick . . . you jumped out ahead of it and then waited for it to catch up. Stopped the barrels again. Take it easy. You've got plenty of time."

"Right."

Thwang.

Bam.

Miss.

And so on until I was getting a little embarrassed what with my wife and a couple of strangers watching this miserable performance. I badly wanted to say that this lah-de-dah skeet-range stuff didn't mean a thing; the acid test was real birds in the field and, by God, I could do all right then, when it counted. My hands were getting sweaty and my heart was starting to beat a little fast. The instructor told me to sit down and take a break. I almost told him to shut up and deal. But I knew him and knew he was all right. So I sat down.

"It's harder than it looks at first," my wife said. "You'll catch on."

Sheer mortification.

I watched while she broke most of the birds that went out in front of her—and watched while a very courtly doctor who'd flown in from the West Coast broke every single bird. I was in bad shape. Then a young woman who was obviously taking the course to please someone other than herself and was just as obviously afraid of guns missed every shot. It should have made me feel better but it didn't. To be in the same category with her was almost insupportable.

On my next time up, I tracked a few birds with an unloaded gun. It felt good and I could sense my timing coming to me. I loaded and when the first bird came out I watched it, pointed at it, kept the barrels moving when I caught and touched the trigger. The bird disappeared in a small puff of coal-colored dust. Ah, yes. Now I have it.

Not quite, of course, since you can't turn anything around that quickly. I missed a few more shots. But I began to feel what I'd done wrong even before the instructor explained it to me. Usually I was stopping the gun. Point and shoot is the way you usually hear the Churchill Method summed up. But those are only two parts of a rather holy trinity, in my opinion. It should be point, shoot, and follow through.

We all got better as the day went on. Everyone except the unfortunate woman who was afraid of guns and doing this because someone had persuaded her to, against her better judgment. She was actually getting worse. I think she was actually closing her eyes. But the instructor never lost patience.

Me, I was getting hotter than the barrels of my old Browning. I wasn't shooting with perfect Churchill form, by any means. My head was too low on the gun, for one thing. The Churchillians want your head almost erect, the better to see your target. But I had shot with my head low for a long time and raising it convinced me that I was shooting under the bird and made me try to compensate until finally I said the hell with it and went back to shooting with my head low. But the rest of it was coming together and, just before lunch, the instructor started throwing doubles for me. The first few went out with a comfortable interval between the birds. I broke about ten doubles in a row. He cut the interval between birds. I kept on them, taking first the bird that came out from my left, breaking it, and then coming back around and taking the bird that came from my right, swinging through and breaking it. I was on a roll.

The instructor tightened up the interval. No problem. People were drifting in for lunch from the other ranges and they had gathered around to watch. That actually made me more confident. *Twang, bam, twang, bam.* Two puffs of sooty smoke on the clear September air. Reload and do it again. I must have gone fifty or sixty straight birds without a miss. For a while there I actually didn't think I *could* miss. I had it. I had it absolutely cold. I was so deep in the groove you couldn't pry me out.

Then the instructor, no doubt aware of my hubris, threw the right bird first. I jumped on it like a startled chicken, shot two feet behind it, then tried to ambush the bird from the left and missed it by twice that distance. Everyone laughed, even me, and we broke for lunch. I had learned more about shooting a shotgun in a morning at that school than I'd learned in my entire life up until then.

I felt great.

And here is my theory for why the Churchill Method works. First, it works because it is close to instinctive. Calculating leads is mental work and you often forget your arithmetic and your vector theory in the heat of a double flush. With the Churchill Method, you don't have to stop and do a lot of thinking. The moves come together with practice, like a good boxer's combinations that he has thrown so often in the gym that, once he is in the ring, he could not stop the follow through punch even if he wanted to.

Next, the Churchill system works because the ranges in most upland bird shooting are not that great and, when they are, the shots are often straight away. So you don't need very long leads, the way you would if you were pass-shooting ducks. The messianic converts to Churchill-style shooting say it works on ducks too but I think I'll stay with calculated leads when you are talking long passing shots.

The third reason I believe the Churchill system works is that there is a lead built into the swing—you simply do not have to calculate it. If you start behind the bird and move the gun to catch up with it and keep moving the gun once you have caught up with it and touched the trigger, then you will be leading the bird when the firing pin strikes the hammer. It takes time for the message to go from eye to brain to hand. Then more time for the trigger finger to make its move. A little more for the mechanical things within the gun to happen. Some more, even, after the primer has exploded but before the shot string leaves the barrel of the gun. We are discussing a very fine fraction of time here, but enough for the gun to be ahead of the bird by a foot or more when the shot leaves the barrel. And at most upland bird shooting ranges, that is enough.

Anyway, the Churchill Method as taught at the Orvis school made me a better shooter. It did not make me a champion but it did make me better. I had a fine season that year. Shooting five hundred rounds on several different ranges two weeks before the season had a lot to do with it. On the darkest day in all of pigeon history, I never shot more than thirty or forty birds. And none of them were flying low and away, the way they could throw some of the clay birds at the school.

We were all better shooters by the time we left—all of us, that is, except the poor young woman who never wanted to shoot in the first place. But even she was having some fun by the time the school was over.

4

Hunting
on the
Reservation

If American sportsmen share any one article of faith, it is probably this—that things ain't as good as they used to be. There was more game in the old days. Bag limits were larger. Less land was posted or developed. People held hunters in better regard. American companies still made fine double guns that a man could buy with a week's wages. And so on and so forth.

All of which is either partly or entirely true. But some things are better. And probably the sportsman who has it best these days is the otherwise busy man who likes to get out now and then for a day of bird hunting but cannot commit a big piece of his life to the enterprise. He does not have a lot of time to scout locations and get permission to hunt on private lands that he thinks will be good when the season comes around. He doesn't have the facilities to keep a good pointing dog or the skill to train him adequately. He knows how to shoot and how to conduct himself in the field. He owns a gun and the proper equipment and he has the desire. But for the rest of it . . . he needs help.

The answer, which is excellent for the beginner as well as for the experienced hunter who is short on time, is the hunting preserve. The game and the dog are there. You pay for the privilege of hunting.

There are all sorts of hunting preserves. Some of them are as exclusive and snooty as Connecticut country clubs and others are corporately owned and managed for executives and their guests and still others are open to the public. What they all have in common is this: they attempt to duplicate the conditions a hunter would find if he could get out and hunt wild birds. The measure of a preserve is how close it comes to this ideal. Some of them do pretty well. Surprisingly well. And not all that do so are private, or totally private, anyway.

The drawback to preserve shooting is also one of its attractions or, rather, one of its selling points. You *know* when you go out that you will find game. You even know how much game you will find. You may find more birds than you have paid for, but never fewer. And that takes something out of the hunt. There is no way around it, unless some preserve were to send hunters out on a dry field every now and then, at random, and then refund their money when they came in, tired and frustrated, at the end of their hunt. It would be a reminder, don't you see. But it would never work.

Still, preserves are a good alternative. The first time I shot on one, I didn't realize that it was planted, so the suspense was still there. I was staying with a friend and we had been up in Canada for a few days of shooting at a lot of purely wild ducks on an Indian reservation. When we got back to his house in the city, he asked if I'd like to go out to his club for some nice dry pheasant hunting. I said sure, imagining that I'd be hunting on private land that was heavily cultivated in some kind of feed that pheasant loved. The feed would not be harvested, so the fields would be full of birds. Club members could shoot a few but the seed birds would be protected. It was a silly vision and the only way I can explain it is to say that I was young.

The next morning we drove out into the country, but not too far—no more than twenty minutes from the last ring of suburban houses that orbited the central city. Just off the highway, down a narrow farm road a mile or two, was a log building with elk antlers nailed above the door. There was a trout pond in front of the cabin and dog kennels off to one side. There must have been a dozen dogs boarded there—everything from German shorthairs to Springer spaniels. The place looked very authentic. We went in and ate a hearty breakfast of meat, eggs, and potatoes off heavy china. Then my host asked a man who was obviously in charge which field was ours for the morning.

"Take the high meadow," he said. "It hasn't been hunted in a while."

"Fine," my host said. He let his young, eager, exuberant Lab out of the back of his station wagon and we walked, perhaps half a mile, through a small woods and came out on about eighty acres of open fields, planted in millet and corn.

"Looks good," I said.

"Oh, it's good all right," my host said, realizing, I think, that I didn't quite know what I was getting into.

"What's the best way to hunt it?" I asked. "Work the edges?"

"Weeelll," my host said, as though giving it some heavy, deliberative thought, "I think we'll just let the dog work through all of it."

"Right," I quickly agreed. "They could still be out feeding on the grain."

"Right."

About thirty seconds after I said that, the Lab started working his nose down close to the ground and his tail began to beat in shortened strokes. He was plainly making game. I started to run to catch up with him. All the wild pheasant I had ever shot out of corn had run ahead of the dog. You had to chase them to make them fly or to be in range when they did fly.

"That's okay. Take it easy," my host said. "Just walk up there and kick around. The bird will come up."

I did what he told me to do and, sure enough, a plump brown hen pheasant came out of the ground cover less than ten yards ahead of me.

"Shoot!" my host shouted.

But I hesitated, since I'd never been where you could legally shoot hen pheasant before. The idea was too new for me to be able to adjust to while the bird was still in range. It flew off absolutely unmolested and put down in the trees.

"We shoot the hens here," my host said.

"Sorry."

"No problem."

"You think that one will run a long way after it hits the ground?"

"These birds seem to stay put," he said.

"Yes, well, I did notice that one held pretty tight for the dog. Not what I'm used to."

By now the Lab was looking gamy again. My host walked up on him and a magnificent cock got up close. My host took his time and got a nice clean kill at about twenty yards. Couldn't have been prettier. Two flushes in less than ten minutes, I thought, and both birds up in easy gun range . . . now *this* is great hunting.

Twenty minutes and three dead birds later, I caught on.

"Uh, say," I said, "these aren't exactly wild birds, are they?"

"Not exactly."

"How often do they put them out?"

"Just before every hunt."

"How many do they put out?"

"Eight. Four cocks and four hens."

"I see. I was just, er, wondering."

My host smiled. "They aren't wild birds, that's for sure. The only thing that acts like a wild pheasant is . . . well, a wild pheasant. And you have to go to North Dakota or Iowa or someplace like that to shoot them. My bad luck I can't just fly out there every weekend."

"Someday, maybe."

"Right. And in the meantime, these may not be wild birds, but they are better than no birds at all. And it's a great way to give the dog some work."

"I'm not complaining."

"I understand."

"It's just that it's . . . ah, *different*."

"Absolutely."

"But still a hell of a lot of fun."

"You don't have to sell me. Just go up there and shoot that bird."

So, to contribute to the feeling of authenticity that I suppose I felt the hunt needed, I walked up and missed a fat going-away cock pheasant with both barrels.

———————•———————

Since that day, I have hunted several other preserves. Some a little better and some a little worse. I would still rather hunt wild birds than planted birds. But I would rather hunt planted birds than no birds at all. And I have found that people who haven't hunted much, but are eager to learn, do better on planted birds in relatively gentle terrain. Also, young dogs can learn a lot in the last few days before the season opens if they get a chance on some planted pheasant or chukars or quail. I've learned, too, that my friends who tie flies are happy to take feathers from planted pheasant—and that they taste just fine.

Also: I have found that pen-raised birds are not bold and re-sourceful like wild birds. They tend to sit still and hope for the best once they have been turned out into the fields. This is all right in good weather. They'll fly readily enough then—though not so readily as a wild bird. But when the weather is cold and wet, the birds on many hunting preserves often will not fly at all. In a situation like that, you are almost better off forfeiting your deposit and staying home to watch football on television. It does, finally, take all the fun out of it if you have to kick the birds to make them fly. And it can happen in bad weather.

If you do not own a dog, by all means ask the preserve to let you hunt with one of theirs. Usually this means they will send someone along to handle the dog. This is all right, too, since with someone else's dog the pleasure is in watching. And if you enjoy bird hunting it is a genuine, deep pleasure that begins to outstrip just about all the other pleasures of the sport. You get to the point where you think you would rather go without a gun than without a dog. Many of the preserve dogs are *very* good. In fact, some of the preserves have breeding operations and, if you have hunted behind a dog you particularly like, maybe you can buy one of its pups.

I suspect that in the future, more and more hunters who find themselves captives of the city and their jobs will turn to preserves for their sport. Simple economics of time will demand it. And I also suspect that the preserves will get larger and better and that some of them will find ways to plant birds that will not be shot within a few hours after they are out of the pen. The problem now is with predators. One preserve where I hunt now and then has a resident population of hawks like nothing I have seen anywhere else in the United States. Any bird that a hunter misses will be a meal for a hawk an hour or two later. But as the preserves get larger and the operations become more sophisticated, I suspect means will evolve that ensure some survival of holdover birds.

As the preserve operations become better, the pressure on the remaining wild-bird habitat might also ease. Which means that they will benefit all bird hunters in the end, not only those who are pressed for time but those who still want to see a dog work and a bird flush in front of the gun. Preserves are a necessary and inevitable part of the times.

5

Gentleman Bob
Bobwhite Quail

Quail hunting is the most orthodox form of bird hunting. The rituals are treasured and passed on and no serious hunter would think of deviating from them. Quail behave in a largely predictable way and so the men and dogs who hunt them are expected to act predictably as well. Each has a role in this small, recurring, and ritualistic drama and none is forgiven unorthodox actions, least of all the hunter.

It starts with the bird itself, the southern bobwhite quail *(Colinus virginianus)*. This little partridge is one of the smallest birds an American bird hunter will shoot. (Snipe and dove are actually a little smaller.) It will weigh about seven ounces and fit nicely in the palm of your hand. It's half the size of a ruffed grouse.

It is a bird of habit, like most game birds, and also a bird that likes companionship. During hunting season, bobwhites are found in coveys of a dozen or more birds. Now and then you will see much larger coveys but fourteen is about average and seventeen is optimum. They gather like this for the common defense—and because a covey will roost in a rough circle or disc at night and fewer than seven birds will not provide the warmth that each needs to make it through the night.

In the morning, after the dew has dried, the covey will move from nesting cover to a feeding area where it will feed until each bird fills its crop. This can take time in a bad year or it can be done in fifteen minutes if conditions are right. Once this morning feeding is accomplished the birds return to cover and may actually nap in the

heat of the day. They will begin feeding again in midafternoon, and toward evening they will return to the roost. Birds of habit, indeed.

When a covey is feeding, most of the birds stay close together but a few drift out a few feet to act as scouts. When a predator comes close, the scout flies and the covey follows.

But flight is a last resort. The bobwhite is not a great flier. One or two hundred yards at a burst would be about its standard range. More importantly, it is camouflaged as well as anything in nature. The back feathers are hued in several shades of brown, some dark as river-bottom mud and some as light and tawny as broom sage. Unless the bird moves, it is impossible to see one in normal cover even when you are fifteen feet away.

So quail hold. They hold for the dogs and, when the dogs have struck a point, they will hold until the hunters walk in and flush them. Then, on the covey rise, the shooting starts.

But as every bird hunter knows, the shooting is much less than all there is to it. What comes before is as important and for some hunters, even more important. If coveys were marked with surveyors' stakes and you walked up to them to flush the birds, so that dogs were not required, then an awful lot of bird hunters would give it up for golf.

Quail hunting gives the hunter an unequaled opportunity to watch and admire the work of his dogs. And it gives the dogs a chance to show what they are made of. Dog work is indispensable to quail hunting and a large population of field-trial competitors and spectators have made the sport strictly a transaction between dogs and birds. Nobody tries to kill any birds. The point is . . . the point. And once that has been accomplished, the flush is merely something that has to be gotten out of the way so that the dogs will leave that covey and go on to another.

Quail hunting yields good dog work because the birds, as mentioned earlier, will hold. Quail generally do not run away from danger—though some oldtimers swear that they do now more than they used to and blame it on the introduction of some fugitive genes into the brood stock. You are always hearing somebody complaining about how "them damned Mexican quail is driving my dogs crazy. Found six coveys today and ever one of them flushed wild." If the birds are a little wilder than they used to be, it is either because they have been hunted more and are skittish or because the ground cover is sparse from modern cultivation. No biological evidence has been produced to back up the "Mexican quail" theory.

And, for that matter, the birds are not *that* wild. They still fly as a last resort and they will almost always hold their ground long enough for a dog to make the scent and then go on point.

Furthermore, the terrain that favors bobwhites also favors the big, ranging dog. It is also usually open enough for the hunter to watch him work. The southern states are best for bobwhites, though they do range out into the Midwest. But the Piedmont sections of the Confederate states are what most hunters think of when they think of quail-hunting country. Rolling hills, growing in second-growth slash pine or even long leaf. Perhaps loblolly, especially up as far as the Carolinas. On the ground, there will be broomweed and lespedeza. Some palmettos, if you are far enough south. The low places will be thick with cyprus and occasionally there will be an old oak standing up on a hillside like a monument to some hard-riding Rebel cavalryman. There will be farming, which provides food for the mature birds, corn being a favorite. There will also be abundant insect life since bugs are an important source of protein for the young birds. It is the sort of land where there might have been some cotton growing more than a hundred years ago. Where they cut the trees for turpentine in the early part of this century. And where they now grow the pine on a fast cycle for pulp. And where, through the evolutions in land use, the bobwhite quail has made itself a home.

You can walk this country. Most hunters do. Or you can ride a horse or a jeep or even sit in style high up on a wagon pulled by a team of mules. However you move, your view will be clear enough that you can watch the dogs as they range out ahead. Most hunters like to have a pair of big dogs on the ground. Hard running setters or pointers. They like to watch the dogs covering ground and then, suddenly, make game and come to that posture of perfect and frozen concentration when they are on point. The one dog actually scenting the birds and the other honoring his point, on sight.

Because the bobwhite is such a bird of the civilized world, man has learned an awful lot about him and, therefore, how to make life better for him. Man has learned, in short, to ensure not merely the bird's survival but its relative abundance.

There was a time when things did not look so good. After the Second World War, when agriculture changed from small patch farms to larger holdings where fields were clean-cropped and marginal land was turned into pasture, the population of bobwhites seemed destined to decline steadily.

Forestry practices contributed their share to this doleful trend. The piney woods that had once been wild stands of uneven aged trees, and were treated as virtually an open range, were managed for maximum production. In the old days, fire had been used to clear the understory so that livestock could move around freely and eat the young green shoots that grew up quickly after fire had cleared the rough.

But the new thinking precluded fire and it went in for large clear cuttings with closely spaced replantings. So the undergrowth was either too thick where it was not burned, or it was nonexistent where the closely spaced pines created an overstory and no sunlight got through to the ground to nourish the herbaceous plants that provide quail with food and cover. Populations, therefore, declined.

But research into the life cycle of the quail and the habitat it required changed some of this. Perhaps the most active and accomplished of the researchers was Herbert Stoddard, whose work *The Bobwhite Quail: Its Habits, Preservation, and Increase* is widely regarded as a classic, while its author is included in that small pantheon of men whose work has changed the way we think about the natural world—men like Aldo Leopold and Gifford Pinchot.

Stoddard, and those who came after, recognized many things

about the relationship of quail to their habitat. Some of them, especially Stoddard's discoveries about fire, were heretical. He recognized that fire was important to the birds and to the trees. And that to exclude fire from the piney woods was to make it harder for both hunters and loggers. The bird needs fire to clear out the understory. Cover can be too thick and a dense bed of pine needles will trap seeds and make it difficult for the birds to get at them. Too much understory will also keep small pine saplings trapped in the grass. Also, pine trees are more fire resistant than some of the hardwood species they compete with. The pine is the desirable species from a logger's point of view, so controlled burning, done at the right time of year and in the proper manner, can be good for quail and foresters. This was a wildly controversial thesis when Stoddard first introduced it but it is widely accepted and burning is almost universally practiced across the South today. The burning takes place in the spring when the coveys are beginning to break up but before the birds have nested. The young will hatch in the summer, then disperse and join up with several different ad hoc groups of birds before finally settling, in the late fall, into the covey that will carry them through the winter.

Managers, especially on private holdings but increasingly on land held by timber companies as well, recognized that a mix in the land was required. Good nesting cover—which is fairly thick ground cover along a border of relatively open ground—must be present and they use machinery to bring about this effect. Lanes are cut through the rough before burning. These will grow back quickly and offer cover. Additional edges are created by planting strips of trees between planted fields and allowing volunteer species of vegetation to grow between the trees and the cleared fields.

Food is obviously a consideration for quail so, if a managed holding is going to contain some cropped fields, then they will be planted in something that makes good food for quail. Corn, especially. Or browntop millet. And other, non-agricultural foods will be introduced where they are not already present as volunteers. Bicolor lespedeza. Beggarweed. Partridge peas.

Land that is well managed for quail will have stands of spaced mature pines. They may all be of the same age or, better, of uneven age, selectively cut, allowing the sunlight to come through the tops and reach the ground.

A well-managed quail-hunting plantation will result in an optimum number of birds, which is about one per acre with covey size averaging about seventeen birds. This can be achieved, and often is, on well-managed holdings where all the tools are used and the land is constantly monitored so that conditions are right throughout the year and food is sufficient, nesting cover is adequate, and some dense protective cover exists.

Of course, even if everything is done according to the latest findings of managers and researchers, there will still be bad years. Too much rain can shut down nesting in the spring. A dry, hot summer can make incubation and hatching difficult. Predation can suddenly increase. Nest predation accounts for the most serious losses and can be expected to run at about 80 percent in a typical year. But it is true that enough is known about the habitat requirements of the bobwhite that it is possible to manage land to ensure high populations on a sustained basis. This is being done on the plantations and, more and more, especially in the use of fire, on the large timber holdings. All of which is good news for the birds—and for the hunters.

———— • ————

People who hunt quail take it seriously. Quite a few make a life of it—not in the sense of becoming "professional quail hunters" (thanks be to God that there is no such thing) but in the sense that hunting quail becomes a lifetime study and avocation for them. It is the part of their lives that they care the most about. They are like passionate amateur astronomers that way, men who will get through a long day of unrewarding work so they can come home to the night and the telescope and the endlessly fascinating heavens.

Likewise, there are bird hunters who exist nine months of every year in order to *live* for three. These are the sort of men who, when the old man in Robert Ruark's *The Old Man and the Boy*, announces that he is mortally ill but promises not to die before opening day of bird season . . . well, they understand exactly.

I think you have to start young to get that way. My favorite quail-hunting companion did. He still likes to talk about coming home from school when he was a boy, putting up his books, and changing from his school clothes to his hunting clothes. He would pick up his gun and get on his bicycle and ride down the main street of the little Alabama town where he was growing up, with his setter named Buck barking and running circles around him all the way out of town. "People would hear that barking and know that it was me, gone out to hunt those little patch farms the sharecroppers ran north of the L & N tracks. I couldn't have snuck out to do it if my life was at stake. Lord, that dog could bark."

He learned that way. On an old Fox double that he probably paid twenty-five or thirty dollars for and that he could still take out and shoot today. When he started, the South was in big stands of timber and small, marginal farms. The place to hunt was where the farms bordered on the woods. "The way people farmed back then, there was always a lot on the ground. I don't know if it was that they were lazy—some of them sure were—or if the equipment wasn't any good—and some of it sure wasn't—or if it was just that people weren't paying such close attention to every dime—because they sure weren't. But, whatever the reason was, there was a lot on the ground around those little farms for the birds to eat. So that's where Buck and I went. I'd get permission to hunt and I'd be out working the edges of those fields every afternoon during the season. Came home every night after dark."

He learned that way, as a boy, and he learned things that are easier to learn when you are a boy than when you are grown, even though that is when they really come in handy.

"The dog and I were both young and we hadn't had much training. We were eager, more than anything else. We made the kind of mistakes you make when you are eager. But the dog was my pet so I never really took it out on him when he busted a covey just because he was running too fast and not paying close attention. I was like a lot of boys and couldn't make myself really lay into a dog for making a mistake. I got enough whippings myself and I didn't think I deserved most of them. So I didn't whip my dog. Still don't."

Perhaps because the dogs are big and strong and tough, a lot of quail hunters are very hard on them when they make a mistake. Some hunters carry a leather strap that they use for whipping dogs and they expect to use it every time out. Some men hunt a dog that wears a shock collar. If the dog makes a mistake, he gets a jolt. Some hunters merely scream a lot. And there are a few who don't mind taking a shot at a dog now and then, presumably when it is far enough away that the shot will merely sting and not penetrate the skin.

"That setter loved to hunt. I didn't have to drag him out in the afternoon when I came home from school. I just treated him like my partner in the thing. He'd run away sometimes, but I didn't yell. I'd just wait a while and he'd come back. I found out then that the less you yell, the quicker a dog will come back. If he hears you yelling, then he knows where you are and he can take his time about coming back to you. If you treat the dog like he's your partner—and that dog slept on the floor of my room and even on the bed when I thought I could get away with it—then it doesn't want to get too far away from you. I don't think I'd thought all this through, back then. I just didn't like yelling at my dog. And the dog still found birds."

Another thing he learned when he was a boy, shooting the old Fox double, was how to hit birds on the covey rise. It is one of the immutable truths of quail hunting that the beginner will simply point his gun in the general direction of the covey when it comes off the ground and shoot, thinking (if it can be called that) there are so many birds in the air that it would be impossible to throw a rock and miss them all, much less shoot a pattern of small shot in their direction and not cut a feather. Every quail hunter has to learn how to pick one bird out of the covey and stay on it until after he has made his shot and that bird is on the ground. The usual pattern is to fire the first shot without aiming and then, when no bird falls, to fire another quickly before the birds have a chance to get out of range.

"Tell you how I learned to take my time on a covey rise. It was economics."

"Huh?"

"Economics. Which, any good economist will tell you, is the study of scarcity. I grew up during the Depression and of all the things that were scarce, one of the scarcest was shotgun shells for young boys. I'd be allowed to take six with me when I'd go out in the afternoon. Sometimes I'd have shot them all before the dog and I had finished the first field. It was a combination of things. But mostly I think it was the pure, blind panic I'd feel when a covey of birds got up, seemed like right from under my feet. Lord. Birds everywhere. And the noise they made. I'd be thinking all the way into where the dog was pointing that this time I was going to keep cool and calm and not go all to pieces when the birds came up . . . then twenty of them would come out of the grass like little brown rockets, making that noise, and I'd panic. Every time.

"Then, one day after I'd shot my six shells without putting anything on the ground, and I was kicking myself for going to pieces on every covey rise, the dog took another point. You couldn't call him off a point. He'd stay there on those birds from now on. So I had to walk in on them to get them to fly, before the dog would come home with me. I carried my gun just like I was going to shoot, even though I couldn't. And when I got up close, the covey flushed. It was still loud and it still startled me a little. But not like before. I watched the birds coming up and then spreading out to fly for a cyprus pond down in a low place just off this little branch. I could almost count the number of birds in the covey, they seemed to be flying so slow. I took my time and picked one out and then I tracked it with my gun and when I caught up with it, I said 'bang.' I almost expected to see that bird fall."

He walked up on other pointed birds with an empty gun and gradually he lost his awe for the covey rise. It didn't seem so explosive anymore. You could get off three or four well-aimed shots, he decided, if you just picked them carefully. The birds weren't that fast. They were in range, going straight away, for a relatively long time. It was a case of studying something and learning about it before presuming to hunt it.

"I actually got to be one of those fellows who can pick out two birds crossing and sometimes take 'em both down with one shot. It doesn't happen all the time—the way some fellows say—and you can miss a lot of birds waiting for it to happen. It's a sort of a stunt. But I've done it."

The shooting got easier and other things became important. Most of the farms he hunted were very small, a few hundred acres at the most, and he got to know them very well. He learned that the bobwhite is territorial. You could find a covey in roughly the same place, day after day. You could, therefore, come back and hunt that covey until you had shot every bird. Which he did once or twice.

"Somebody had to speak to me about that. I was so excited and full of myself being able to kill them that I didn't think about down the road. I just liked going out with six shells and coming back with six birds. That seemed as fine as anything could be."

But you need seed birds if there is going to be another covey in the same field, next fall. No hunter can so clearly choose to be a conservationist—or not—the way a quail hunter can. Which adds to the burden of protocol the sport carries.

"Funny, the first time I ever did it—shot every bird in a covey— I felt kind of proud of myself. A mighty hunter, don't you know. I must have been all of fourteen. Maybe less. And back then, well the point was to kill birds. When I was not killing birds I felt like I was wasting those six shotgun shells and wasting those shells was a lot worse in my mind than destroying that covey of birds.

"But I learned. I went back to fields where I had always found birds before, first day or two of the season, and there weren't any birds there. And that was a big disappointment. The covey that was supposed to be in that field, well, it had started to seem like an old friend to me. I missed those birds something bad.

"And when I told another, older bird hunter about it and he asked me if I'd shot the birds out the year before, I said 'yes.' "

"And he said, 'Well, *hail* boy, how do you expect them birds to be there? You figure they're going to just grow out of the ground? A young man your age is bound to know about the birds and bees and all the rest of it. You ought to be able to understand that there's got to be some birds and bees around to do what needs to be done. That's the most important thing.'

"I started leaving seed birds after that. At least four pairs from every covey. Sometimes, if the covey was small and the singles flew out on a big flat ridge where I knew that I could hunt them up easy, I'd let them go. Just take what I'd gotten on the covey rise. I got to be the way I am now, where I feel real proprietary about my birds. I shoot a few and I leave a few and I don't like for other people to come in and shoot behind me, so I don't tell anyone where I hunt. I want to find coveys next year where I've been finding them this year and for a lot of years before that. I'm getting too old to do a lot of prospecting for birds. If they'll just multiply during the off season and come back to the fields where they've always been, then hell . . . I'll just skim a few, less than the foxes and the hawks will take, and we'll call it a bargain."

———————•———————

Aside from being a conservationist and a believer in ritual, the dedicated quail hunter is most likely to become someone who knows more than a little about being a good companion. It is hard to think of anything in sport that is so often done in pairs.

Not with just pickup partners, either. Bird-hunting partnerships tend to be for the long term, even for life, and I'm sure if you could do the survey, it would establish that the average quail-hunting partnership outlasts the average American marriage by a factor of at least four. I don't know why that is but I've heard some theories. The Alabamian I've been talking about started with a friend when they were in high school and the two of them are still at it, three wars, half a dozen children, several grandchildren, and probably fifteen pointer dogs later. The idea of getting out of bed on a Saturday morning, and going out hunting, one without the other, would never occur to either of them. If one didn't call the other, sometime mid-week, to make sure of the arrangements, then somebody would know that somebody else had died.

"I've hunted by myself," the Alabama quail hunter says, "done it quite a bit, in fact, and it ain't bad. Better by a damn sight than not hunting at all. But I prefer to be with a partner and Jack is my partner all these years. I suppose it has something to do with how much time you spend watching the dogs and just walking along behind them. It's nice to have somebody to talk to. You don't talk about anything very important. Fact is, you mostly talk about what the dogs are doing up ahead of you, but it is still nice to have somebody to talk to. Somebody you feel comfortable with.

"Now, I don't like to hunt with any more than one other person. I don't need any three-way conversations. Then, somebody is *always* talking. And I despise that. It's why I won't go on those dove shoots they have. All those people around the field, shouting and carrying on. That isn't hunting to me. But I like to be walking along behind the dogs, on a pretty day, and having somebody to talk to. And somebody to give you a little teasing when you miss a shot. 'That's a mighty bird,' Jack will say after I've missed clean on a single, 'look at the way he can fly with his whole body full of number eight bird shot.'

"And I suppose you like to have someone along when you are out in the woods, just in case something happens. When I was younger, I suppose there was reason to worry I'd get a heart attack. Nothing worries me that much anymore. But I could step in a gopher hole and break a leg and there isn't a pointer dog alive that could drag me a mile back to the car. So safety comes into it. There are snakes where we hunt. Not like there are out in Texas or down in South Florida, but we've got them. I don't worry so much about getting bit myself, but I do worry about the dog. Every now and then, a dog around here will point a diamondback and get bit. Most of them die but now and then you can get one out and to the vet in time. And you couldn't do it if you were hunting alone. So that's part of it.

"But I think it just comes down to the fact that you get used to having somebody along to talk to. And it is something that doesn't keep changing on you, like everything else in this life, so you stick with the partner you've had. The birds act the same, the woods look the same, and your partner is the same. It's just not worth it to break in a new one."

So the partnership becomes part of the ritual along with everything else.

6

The Wild Ones

Ruffed Grouse and Woodcock

As predictable as the bobwhite is, the ruffed grouse is every bit that unpredictable. You can look at the birds, up close, and see that they are biologically related in some distant way. The same dark feathers and bantam body with its plump breast and short neck. They have the same abrupt, hooked beak that helps them with their feeding. The grouse is more than twice the size of the quail and there is no immediate and obvious way to tell a cock from a hen as there is with the quail where the little rooster always shows some white around the head. But still . . . you can tell at a look that these birds are cousins.

But they have taken separate paths and once you get beyond the superficial resemblances, they are as unlike as North and South. Which is, perhaps, the appropriate analogy, even though you can find ruffed grouse as far south as Georgia and quail as far north as southern Minnesota. The overlapping territories are deceiving, however. The quail is a social and proper little bird, a pure product of the South. The ruffed grouse is a solitary eccentric, a resourceful Yankee.

Where the quail will hold, most of the time, the grouse sometimes will and sometimes won't. Which is just the beginning of what he sometimes will and sometimes won't do. When he does flush, the bird will sometimes tower straight up and then, sometimes, he will fly so low to the ground that you think of those terrain-hugging fighter planes and shoot into a patch of steepletop not three feet high. Sometimes the bird will go downhill and then again, sometimes he will fly straight up the mountain. Once he is on the wing, the grouse will sometimes just go and go and then, sometimes, he won't even get out of gun range before he lights in the top branches of a tree. Sometimes he will fly straight and sometimes he will dodge. Sometimes he will hold tight and other times he will flush so wild that you barely get a look at him a hundred yards or more up ahead. Sometimes he will wait until you've gone by and fly out behind you. You never know what the bird is going to do until he has done it. Where it is hunted intensively, in New England and in the upper Midwest, the ruffed grouse is the most challenging bird you can hunt.

He lives in tough country, just for openers. Like the quail, he flies as a last resort but, since he is a loner, he cannot count on the security that comes with numbers. Once the birds of the year have separated it is rare to find more than one grouse. Occasionally you will flush a pair and, very rarely, three or four at a time. But you can easily go a full season and never flush anything but single birds.

———•———

The ruffed grouse has been hunted with enough passion for enough years that a number of beliefs are held about the bird, many of them wrong. The best way to disabuse yourself in advance is to read Gordon Gullion's book *Grouse of the North Shore*, which is the result of years of close and scientific study.

Gullion exposes a number of fallacies, beginning with the belief that the ruffed grouse is a partridge. He then goes on to explain the way that grouse get together in the spring, the male drumming to establish territory and entice the hens. Drumming is accomplished not by the feet or the mouth, as some believe, but by the wings—which the grouse flaps in brutally short strokes to create a vacuum that air rushes to fill, creating the thumping sound. If you've been in grouse country, especially in the spring or fall, you have heard grouse drumming. It sounds something like a chain saw starting up.

Grouse nest in the spring. Once nesting has begun, the male has

no more role, unlike the bobwhite male, which shares nesting duties. Incubation of grouse eggs lasts a little more than three weeks and when the birds hatch, they leave the nest almost immediately and begin to feed on their own, principally on insects. Chicks grow to maturity in about sixteen weeks. When small birds are spotted in the fall by hunters, this is often said to indicate a second nesting. Actually, it indicates that the birds hatched late because the hen lost her first clutch of eggs and renested. There is no evidence that the grouse can raise two successful broods in one season.

The young chicks eat insects through the summer. Insects are protein rich. And there will be some losses if there is enough rain to keep insect populations down. But a wet spring or early summer is not the grouse killer that some hunters believe.

Late in the summer and early in the fall, the broods begin to break up and the young grouse go to those places where hunters will find them when the season starts. Most of the birds he sees will be birds of the year.

In the summer and the fall, food is plentiful and though there are hunters in the field, this is a relatively good time for the grouse. There is good ground cover and a lot of food. Hunters do not account for large numbers of grouse taken, especially in the best habitat—which is dense aspen from about ten to twenty-five years old. These small trees, which grow close and thick, are hard for hunters—and other grouse predators—to move through without giving themselves away. Contrary to popular belief, the celebrated "edge" between cleared and covered land is not a secure home for the grouse. He needs to be deep in the cover of protective aspen, according to Gullion, to reach his optimum population density of ten breeding pairs per one hundred acres. It is in the marginal cover, where birds have taken up recent residence, that losses to predators are at their highest. Hunters included, predators take about 1 percent of the total grouse population per day during this time. But by the end of the hunting season, and the beginning of deep winter, the surviving grouse will be in the well-protected covers.

It is after the hunting season that the grouse faces his time of maximum danger and undergoes the ordeals that account for the famous cycle. A good winter for grouse is one of deep dry drifting snow. The grouse can burrow into the snow for both warmth and protection from predators. In a year when there isn't adequate snow cover or the snow is crusted after a thaw or rain, the grouse is exposed to the cold, which means it must find more food and therefore spend more time vulnerable to the raptors that are its primary predator.

Late in the winter, the grouse depends primarily on aspen buds for food. In years when these are plentiful, life is easier. The grouse can feed in the branches of the male aspen and fill his crop in fifteen minutes or so. The buds are high in protein, which helps the bird maintain body warmth and mass at this crucial time when he is so close to the end.

If, however, the aspen buds are not available, the grouse will have to feed on other foods—often ironwood and birch. It takes several buds from these trees to equal the nutrition of one aspen bud and, worse, the twigs are not as strong so while the grouse is feeding in the branches of these trees, he is flapping his wings, which both expends energy and attracts the attention of goshawks and owls.

It is the availability of the aspen food source that Gullion thinks is primarily responsible for the health of the grouse population entering the breeding season. A weakened population may not produce enough clutches of healthy eggs or may lack sufficient strength in the case of some birds to breed at all. Also, the winter losses will have been greater.

There is one final discovery of his that is of interest to the grouse hunter. The aspens seem at some point to produce a protective covering over the buds that inhibits their digestion by grouse. This blocking of their favorite food may have quite a bit to do with the swings in grouse populations over the years. But as Gullion points out, much remains to be learned. What has been accomplished already is of great help, however, to managers, and therefore to the hunters as well.

———————•———————

The ruffed grouse's first line of defense against his predators is thick cover where he can hide and use his natural camouflage and where the predators either cannot move at all or where they certainly cannot move without making enough noise so that the grouse knows exactly where they are. In the Midwest, they like the places where mixed second growth has been cut over for pulp and the aspen is coming back. The loggers leave the tops and stumps and from the now un-shaded ground, all sorts of vines and briars and ground plants spring up to weave themselves through the dead unwanted limbs. Walking through flat, pulped-over land is as hard as walking uphill. You crash into walls of vegetation that has wrapped itself around the natural trellises of dead treetops and sometimes it is all you can do just to move. It is like fighting the densest rhododendron that ever grew.

But that is where the birds are. For both food and cover. The thick cover gives this erratic bird a choice. He can either hunker down and count on his camouflage to protect him. Or he can run ahead of the hunter, picking his way at ground level. And if all else fails, he can fly—which he does just about the time the hunter is so helplessly tangled in the undergrowth that he can't possibly shoot, much less turn around and shoot since the blasted bird has flushed *behind* him.

In a situation like this, a dog is an option rather than a necessity. Many very good and very serious Midwestern grouse hunters do not hunt with a dog. They believe that a dog, even a good one, will flush as many birds, inadvertently, as it will successfully point, and a man who doesn't mind breaking brush through the tough pulped-over covers will flush as many, or more, birds in range as any dog will. This may or may not be true. But it tells you something about the bird that a lot of men who hunt it seriously think this way. One wonders, however, about the number of crippled grouse that are lost by hunters who do not have a dog to assist them on the retrieve or, indeed, help them find grouse that are lying dead but concealed in the brush.

————————•————————

It is interesting to consider how the grouse became so wary. In some parts of its range, the bird is called a "fool hen" and the locals shoot it on the ground or off the branches of trees, generally using a .22 rifle for the job and shooting for the head. That way you don't damage the meat and if the bird is dumb enough to let you get that close, then what the hell.

You see this in the extreme northern portions of the bird's range. This, not coincidentally, is country where the grouse has never been hunted intensively, the way it was around the Great Lakes and New England states where it was first a staple and then a delicacy, hunted by market gunners who shot thousands of birds every year and considered twenty-five a barely acceptable bag for one day of hunting. The grouse, under this kind of pressure, learned quickly. It was that or perish.

You can see the learning process at work over the course of a single season. Early, when the leaves are still on the trees, and you go into a favorite covert, you are likely to find the birds holding to points, if you are using a dog, and flushing within reasonable gun range. Those you can see clearly you might kill.

But every time a bird is flushed and shot at, it learns something. If you continue to hunt the same covert, through the season, you will notice later in the year that the survivors are almost always flushing wild, well out of range.

One season, not long before I wrote this, I had hunted a covert that is convenient enough that I call it my "home covert," even though I do not own the land. I can get up there late in the day, after work, and get an hour of good shooting and nobody else seems to hunt it. I find a lot of birds there. But this was a poor season. A month into the season, I was convinced that there was only one grouse left in the covert and that I could get a look at him every time I hunted. But getting a shot was something else again.

The bird had flushed wild and out of range a dozen different days and I was beginning to count on it, the way you expect a wise old brown trout to refuse every fly you throw at him. But you go to the pool again and again to try just the same. I was hoping, every time I went up to the home covert, that some new birds would have moved from the hardwoods up on the mountain where I figured they had been eating acorns and beechnuts but risking the wrath of owls and goshawks. As the days got shorter and the ground got barer they would be moving into my home covert, happy to eat the thornapples and aspen buds and hide in the steepletop where the worst they had to fear was me and my dog. And . . . if there were no new arrivals, then that one wise old bird would be in there somewhere, ready to give us another lesson.

I'd become accustomed to his flushing far out of range. In fact, I subtracted points for that kind of performance. It was too easy. I admired it when he would flush from behind a wall of thick ground cover and fly so low that he was always behind a bush. That seemed sporting. And I was especially respectful of the performance he gave when he stood to a point one day when my dog was on one side of a barbed wire fence and I was on the other. He flushed, naturally, when I was straddling the wire.

Then one day, when I had my wife with me, he gave us all a lesson—a demonstration of just how smart a bird with more than a hundred generations of human predation behind him can be.

My dog can trail birds. Every grouse hunter who owns a dog will tell you that, but when I say it, I am telling the truth. My dog can trail. At the junction of two stone walls, in a low spot in the cover, she began to move with slow deliberation, nose close to the ground. She was plainly making game.

But quickly lost the scent.

She came back to where she'd started and tried it again. She went a little farther this time before losing the scent, twenty-five yards out along the stone wall.

This time she got a little frantic. She made a cast back and then out in every direction and still could not pick up the scent. We had not heard or seen the bird flush. Grouse generally come up big, making lots of noise, almost as much as a whole covey of quail. But they can flush silently. They are unpredictable.

I had just about decided that the bird had flushed quietly and flown in to the safety of a plot of planted Christmas trees. I whistled to the dog, who climbed the stone wall to get to my side. She made game on top of the wall.

For the next one hundred and fifty yards, she eased along the wall, stepping carefully from stone to stone, looking as though she might freeze onto a point at any step. My wife took one side of the wall and I took the other. With the dog on top, I did not see how we could fail. Once the dog had stopped the bird, it would have to fly either to my side or my wife's side of the wall. One of us would at least get a shot. We had outsmarted that grouse, I thought, which was much more than half the battle.

I watched the dog. The bird was there. No question about it. Any minute now. We were coming up to the end of the wall. There were three or four birch trees growing there, where the field fell away, down a hundred-foot hill to a tight patch of spruce.

The bird flushed, just about the time I realized exactly how it could be done. He used the birch trees and the drop of the hill so that when he came up big and loud, not thirty steps from either of us, neither my wife nor I ever even *saw* him. He used the trees and the steep pitch of the hill and, before that, the old stone wall, to get away from us one more time. He was still there, in the covert, at the end of the bird season. I know because I put him up when I went up there just looking around, when there were two feet of snow on the ground. He flushed out of range, even though I wasn't carrying anything more lethal than ski poles. I was proud to see he was still there.

———————•———————

It goes almost without saying that it is this craft and intelligence that make the grouse such a pleasure to hunt. The grouse hunter never has to worry about shooting down the brood stock. He can literally shoot as many grouse as the law allows and still be an indifferent threat as far as the survival of the species is concerned. The fewer birds there are, the smarter they will be. This has been established scientifically on similar plots of ground with identical populations of birds. One was hunted, intensively, by old market hunters, while the other was not hunted at all. The hunters killed birds, of course, but after a while the remaining grouse were flushing wild or carefully and by the end of the experiment both plots of ground held about the same number of birds. The hunters were doing the work of other predators and once a certain point had been reached, the native wariness of the bird ensured its survival.

So we are not dealing here with an easy kill. Which is one very big reason for the fact that many hunters prefer other birds to grouse. The phrase "serious grouse hunter" is almost a redundancy. Some men will go out with an untrained dog and poke around the edges of likely grouse cover and say that they are hunting. But they aren't and probably they know it. The real grouse hunter dives into that thick cover and stays in there until he has hunted it out. He goes in there in full knowledge of the fact that he may not find any birds or, more likely, the ones that he does find will flush wild or from behind too much cover for him to get a shot, or flush when he has just stuck a thorn into his eye and cannot see to shoot because it is watering so badly. He knows that it will not be an unusual day when he flushes ten birds and sees only half of them and doesn't get a single clear shot.

———•———

Some of the frustration of grouse hunting can be eased by the presence, in some of the same habitat, of woodcock. This is a smaller bird with a long needlelike beak for punching the soft ground in search of earthworms. The woodcock is a prize game bird in its own right and many hunters go after it alone and consider the occasional grouse the bonus. Woodcock and grouse cover overlap or lie adjacent to each other. The woodcock likes softer, wetter earth as a rule, but rules are made to be broken and, in some coverts, you are never sure exactly what is going to come up in front of your dog. A big noisy grouse boring away low, or a towering woodcock, its primary feathers giving off a single high squealing note as it pitches almost straight up before leveling out to try to put some distance between itself and whatever forced it to fly.

Woodcock are present in many areas as resident birds but they also migrate down the length of the United States, coming over from Canada where they are abundant. These flight birds usually move ahead of a cold front and in one day a thick alder covert can go from holding one or two birds to holding ten times that many. As the moving birds stop to rest up, the hunter can find all the action he needs. And action is sometimes a tonic for the frustrated grouse hunter who would like to get a nice strong point from his dog and a good look at something he can shoot. The cover is as tough for woodcock— and sometimes tougher—as for grouse. But the birds tend to hold to

a point so you can get close and get a look even if the thick branches make for problematic shots.

When the flight birds are in, you can sometimes see the bore holes where they have been driving their beaks into the ground. And you can surely see the white droppings, which hunters call "chalk."

When you have found chalk, in a wide, low plain filled with alders, say, you can give your dog and yourself a real workout. The birds will hold for a point and, in my experience, a dog that has trouble on other game birds still might do well on woodcock. Perhaps this is because the woodcock puts out more and stronger scent or because, once pointed, it does not tend to move and get the dog all confused. Still, the dog can often get close enough to see the bird that it is pointing; this is usually trouble but not with woodcock. What it all comes down to is that woodcock are made to be hunted with dogs and, when there are a lot of birds around, a hunter will get a fine chance to admire his dog while he performs.

A hunter who tries woodcock without a dog will have problems. He will walk right past a number of birds since they hold so tight and he will not be able to find a fair number of the birds that he does manage to flush and knock down. The woodcock is small and darkly hued and you can almost step on a dead bird, lying in the leaves, before you will see it. Even if your dog will not retrieve woodcock (and some find the smell just too strong to be willing to put that thing in their mouths) it will certainly point dead birds so that you can do the actual retrieving.

The shooting is another lure to the hunter when the flight birds are in. Any bird hunter with a proper ration of pride likes to think he is *quick*—that he can get the gun up and get the shot off just as fast as he needs to and still be deadly. Nothing will test that pride like woodcock in tough cover. The birds themselves are not fast, nor do they fly nimbly. But they do fly through the *damnedest* stuff and to be a really good gun on woodcock, you have to be able to point and shoot. The skeet man who takes leisurely, sustained leads will be in deep trouble in a choked woodcock covert.

During hunting season you will often find woodcock in pairs and it is then that you can put your gunning to a genuine test. Finding the first bird and bringing it down, and then locating the second, moving the gun sufficiently to cover it, and, finally, shooting it is the kind of accomplishment that would get your picture in the papers if journalists really understood what constitutes an achievement in this world. In many ways, a double on woodcock is probably the most difficult piece of business a hunter can accomplish, at least from a gun-handling point of view.

The arrival of the flight birds is always welcome news. The woodcock is hardy and there will be birds moving south in great numbers every year. On the midwestern flyway (where about 75 percent of the woodcock are concentrated) the birds are as abundant as ever, while in the East there have been difficulties recently. The woodcock is tough and does not suffer to any excessive degree from predation. Pesticides can be a problem for the woodcock, since the worms it eats tend to concentrate these poisons and the woodcock only furthers the process. The bird is hurt most severely by weather, especially a hard freeze on its winter grounds. If it cannot get its beak into the ground, the woodcock is in trouble. When there has been a significant loss of birds, the federal government might adjust season dates along the flyway to reduce the number taken by hunters.

The male woodcock is smaller than the female and the flight birds usually have more subcutaneous fat, which becomes evident when you clean them. They are hunted up and down the eastern seaboard from Maine to Louisiana and they are noble, game little birds. It is a good day when you find the flight birds in some grouse cover and come home with a mixed bag of woodcock, ruffed grouse, and memories.

———————•———————

The grouse hunter can measure how good the season has been by how many pairs of briar-proof pants he has ripped beyond repairing. Three or four pair means that he has been out a lot. Therefore, he will have seen some birds and gotten some shots. If he is still wearing the same pair of briar-proofs he started the season with, then he must not have gotten out much. Maybe he was too busy, in which case other grouse hunters will hope, sympathetically, that he made a lot of money.

So what is it about grouse hunting that makes it so seductive? Why do the hunters who concentrate on grouse look forward to the two months of bird season so intensely that they can honestly say it is the time of year when they feel most alive? Isn't it an awful lot of trouble, bordering on the masochistic, for a very slender payoff?

Well, in the first place, being hard doesn't disqualify something from being rewarding or even pleasant. Grouse hunters remember tough covers the way climbers remember tough mountains—affectionately. And it isn't all torn clothes and birds flushing out of range or invisible behind the steepletop. There are those other days, when the weather is good, with the sky clear and the air cool and the wonderful rich colors of autumn everywhere on the land. You get the day to hunt and go to your favorite covert, which you have kept a secret from everyone except your hunting partner. (Grouse hunters are psychotically protective of their coverts. They will park a mile away from where they actually intend to hunt so that other hunters will not decide to give an area a look once they have recognized the car.)

There were several days like that last year but one of them I remember better than the others—I suppose because it was fairly late in the season, coming up on opening day for deer, which is a good time to stop grouse hunting.

I was walking up the old logging trace to my best covert an hour or so after breakfast. The dog was running ahead, wearing the small copper cow bell that I put on her collar when we are going out. Without the bell, I wouldn't know where she is half the time. As it is, I still lose track of her now and then, especially when she goes on point. On several occasions, she has held for ten minutes or so and then barked to tell me where she was.

She was in thick aspen and birch before I was to the top of the hill but I could still hear the bell. I was walking slowly, taking in the view of the little farm valley below me and the line of mountains standing out in clear relief on the horizon. When I got to the top of the hill, I looked around for the dog and didn't see her. Then I listened for the bell. The only sounds came from some scattered songbirds and a distant chainsaw that somebody was putting to hard use, no doubt hoping to finish up on the woodpile before the first serious snowstorm of the winter.

I stopped and strained to hear the bell. Nothing.

I called, "Molly." Sometimes she will stop and wait for me and, because she is small, even for a Brittany, I won't see her. She will almost always move when she hears her name. Unless she is on point. She did not move this time; there was no sound of a bell. Only the chainsaw and, now, the audible sound of my heart, which always beats faster when a dog goes on point—even if I can't see it.

I walked into the small trees where I'd last seen her and, after a minute or two of looking, I saw her standing rigid in a point. Her lips were curled back from her teeth and quivering. Her nose was twitching. She did not look back at me even though she must have known I was there.

I walked in and the bird flushed. I threw the gun to my shoulder on the sound of the flush and the bird and the gun barrel seemed to come into a perfect alignment almost without any help from me. You have to get that way when you shoot grouse. When I touched the trigger, the bird crumpled. The dog, which starts every season trained to hold to wing and shot, broke and picked up the dead bird and brought it back to me. I had long since lost any desire to scold her.

"Good work, Molly," I said and took the bird from her. "Good work. I think we're both hot today."

I studied the bird. There is nothing gaudy about a grouse. It is all dark colors: greys and browns with some black thrown in. But it is, a lot of us think, one of the most handsome birds in nature. The shadings of color are dark and dignified. There is an overall richness to the various dark hues; a richness that is both beautiful and functional.

I spread the tail and studied the black band at the tip of the feathers. It was broken, slightly, in the middle—which meant the bird was probably a hen. The band is usually continuous on the male birds, but there is no sure way of determining the sex of the bird in the field. This bird was large and plump but I couldn't say for sure if it was a bird of the year or an older, carryover bird since it was so late in the season and there had been so much food. But the odds were it was this season's bird. Few grouse make it all the way through a year. Twenty percent is a high survival rate. No bird lives to be older than five.

I checked the crop on this bird. It was full of thornapple. I had also found fox grapes, beechnuts, aspen buds, and chokecherries in the crops of birds I'd killed from this covert. Those are just a few of the seventy or eighty different foods they like. One year, when a late frost had killed the apples, the birds in our part of the country ate the hophorn mast that was abundant.

I put the bird in my game pouch and followed the impatient dog farther into the cover. The sky was still blue but off to the west, where most of our hard weather originates, there was a gauzy blur forming on the horizon. The temperature seemed to be holding just when the day should have been warming. Many hunters have noticed that some of their best days come when a cold front is moving in, bringing a storm. The birds seem to know they need to fill their crops and the scenting conditions are ideal for the dogs: warm ground and cool air, so the scent tends to stay on the ground, trapped almost by the arriving cold.

The dog ran ahead. We were coming to a flat field, open enough that the blackberry briars had found sun and taken root. The dog and I both hated this place almost as much as the birds seemed to like it. I made all the usual signals, indicating to the dog that I wanted her to dive in and check out those briars. She looked at me like she thought I was either joking or crazy—when you own a dog, it is amazing how many expressions you can recognize in its face—and stuck to the perimeter of the field where small aspens and maple grew thick and stunted.

So, I pushed into the blackberry briars and the dog, reluctantly, followed. She was sure, by this time, that I was crazy but I was her hunter so she had to go along. She made a hard point about ten minutes later. I walked up to her but the bird had run. She started trailing and I followed her, absolutely oblivious to the briars that were so high they tore the skin of my neck.

The dog moved a few steps, stopped, then took another cautious step or two, stopped and, almost at the same time, the bird came up big and loud, twenty steps ahead. It was almost to the alders when I knocked it down with my second shot.

It was one of those clean, lucky kills. There was less blood on this bird than there was on the dog, or me for that matter. I think one or two stray pellets from the pattern caught the bird in the head. But I wasn't complaining.

On the way up a large hill that is thick on one side with hophorn and on the other with thornapples, we passed through the remains of a small orchard, abandoned along with the farm that had once occupied this land and where a family had once pastured sheep, tapped trees for syrup, and picked a few apples. I picked one from a tree that was full of rot and badly needed pruning but was still capable of producing some fruit after twenty years of neglect. The apple was spotted and badly formed, unacceptable for the market, but it tasted just fine in the biting morning air.

We found a straggling woodcock in the hornbeam. The flight birds had passed through almost a month earlier and we had found plenty of them. But there had been two big cold fronts through since then and most of the woodcock were probably safe in Louisiana by now. This one had stayed on. The dog pointed hard as stone.

The bird came up all legs and wings, rising for the first twenty feet or so like it was being lifted on a string. Then it leveled out and started to fly downhill. It was an easy shot. The dog went over to the dead bird but wouldn't pick it up. Woodcock are too strong for her. They use their long, needlelike beak to probe the soft earth of alder thickets and eat the worms they find there. Their flesh is dark and gamy, too rich for some tastes. I think of woodcock as small ducks and would rather eat them than grouse. My dog does not agree.

So I did my own retrieving and then started back up the hill. The sky was growing lower and thicker and a wind had picked up strength in the two hours we'd been out. There would be a storm that night. Maybe sooner. Maybe for that reason, the dog and I both hunted with a little more urgency, pushing ourselves on up the hill. The unseen man on the chainsaw was pushing himself, too. The engine never stopped.

At the top of the hill, where it flattened out into a long gentle slope, there were thornapples and, aspens and, in the clear places, steepletop as high as your waist. Good grouse cover. Hard on the clothes but not as bad as the briars had been. A bird got up ahead of us, wild and out of range. When the dog found the scent, she would not leave it alone. There was a bird around there somewhere, dammit—she knew there was. She could *smell* it. Finally, I convinced her to give it up and come along.

The sun was gone, obscured by a scudding grey sheet that was not a cloud but a gathering of clouds, the forward edge of a serious storm. The temperature had fallen and the back of my shirt, which was wet with perspiration, felt cold against my skin. We should be getting back to the car.

But we decided—and I say *we* advisedly because the dog clearly had an opinion and I had to respect it—to finish out the thornapples since they had been good to us before.

And, just as the first drops of frozen rain hit my face, they were good to us again. The dog started trailing and I trotted to catch up with her. She stopped and I went in. The bird flushed very low and seemed actually to be flying down some kind of alley in the steepletop. I waited until it was out over bare ground and shot it cleanly. I didn't take time to study this one but slipped it into the pouch and started back for the car. My vest felt satisfyingly heavy, the way a prospector's gold pouch would feel after a good day on his claim. The dog, who would now and then heel, stayed right with me. She seemed to know. We stayed on an old sunken logging trace all the way back through the covert, passing up places that we knew were good. The temperature had fallen more than ten degrees since we'd been out. Felt like twenty but that didn't seem possible. When we were a quarter of a mile from the car, the rain turned to snow. It was falling in thick wet flakes and my hands were numb when I opened the door.

The car heater was a blessing and I felt warm driving back down to the main highway and, then, on to the house. Warm and charitable. This was the way the season ought to end. The dog had performed and so had I. Three birds with a woodcock bonus. Not a lot of wild flushes or impossible shots, especially for this late in the season. It was the last day, in fact, though technically you could shoot for another month. Hardly anyone did, once the snow got deep.

So I had a good day to carry me through until next season, when the leaves started turning and the nights started turning cool. And the deer hunters, I thought, could use this tracking snow. It doesn't work out this way all the time, of course. Not even very often.

Only just enough.

7

Other Birds, Other Times

*Pheasants, Sharptail Grouse,
Hungarian Partridge, Chukar,
Desert Quail*

All upland bird hunting can be described as falling somewhere between hunting for bobwhite and hunting for grouse, since those birds represent the extremes. But first you must admit to a definition of upland bird hunting, which goes this way: the hunter is on the ground, almost always with a dog, and he is moving. He may get wet but he is not hunting over water and, even if he is not using a dog (rare), he is on the move and not waiting for the birds to come to him as in, say, dove shooting.

This, of course, eliminates the great driven shoots of England and the continent. An awful lot of bird hunting lore and ritual comes from this tradition, but even those who practiced it were careful to make the distinction. When they walked they were hunting and when the birds and other game were driven in to them by beaters, it was shooting.

They must have been something, the shoots and the shooters. Thousands of birds would be killed in a single day by the guests at one of those shoots. Every shooter carried at least two guns and was accompanied by a loader so that he did not have to waste time, or miss birds, for the mere nuisance activity of loading his gun. According to some accounts, a man of that time was considered a good shooter if he could manage to have three dead birds in the air at once. Which sounds like a gross exaggeration until you begin to look into the accounts of those days. One man, a Lord Roper, once had seven dead birds in the air at one time. He also shot twenty-eight pheasants once, in the space of a single minute.

————— • —————

But that was a different age. The Edwardians were the last of the naive optimists (which is a close definition of enlightenment) and they did what they did in the firm conviction that there was absolutely nothing wrong with it. These days, no hunter would shoot one hundred birds in a day, even if he could. And if he did, he certainly would not brag about it to his peers. Which the Edwardians did with relish.

The great driven shoots and shooters are described faithfully and charmingly in a little book called *The Big Shots* by Jonathan Garnier Ruffer. He describes, in vivid and witty detail, the house parties that were adjuncts to the shoots. The exquisite manners and childish fascinations of the nobles who attended them. And the extraordinary number of birds they killed. There is an account of one shooter who left an estate before the shoot began, telling his host by note, "I am leaving because the entree was so cold at dinner it made my teeth ache all night." Another accidentally shot a lady guest's dachshund and when she made a scene about it, proceeded to have the dog stuffed and mounted and then sent it to her encased in glass. And then there was the shooter who once killed 1,070 grouse in fourteen hours. On a bet, evidently. In the introduction to the Ruffer book, this man's nephew describes him thusly:

His Lordship's framed grouse record now hangs in the lavatory at Merton Hall—the decision of the hanging committee being more influenced by his later financial unsuccess than by any intrinsic flaw in its design. He gambled heavily on converting Walsingham House in Piccadilly into a club and hotel [now the Ritz Hotel] and his debts eventually led to the breaking of the entail on his estates and the relative impoverishment of his posterity. His marital infidelities also were remarkable, in an age when infidelity was commonplace; though the scandal was for the most part confined to the locality since it seems he usually slept with his housemaids. He left no legitimate issue.

The tradition endures in vastly more modest fashion. There are still driven shoots, especially in England and Scotland, and the look of the sport is carried on in the Barbour wax-treated cotton foul-weather gear that was designed for driven shoots over damp moors and has now become something of a fashion item.

Driven shoots never took in this country, which grieves some Anglophiles, but the truth is that America has neither the terrain nor the temperament for them. Driven shoots were possible because of the great, well-tended estates that were run precisely for the shooting and because the law limited hunting to the nobility by making game the property of the landowner. In America the land is farmed—and hunted—democratically.

So the bird hunter actually hunts, and if he can hunt bobwhite and grouse, then any other bird he hunts will fall somewhere in between those two in terms of temperament and behavior. The quail is gregarious and proper while the grouse is solitary and eccentric. In between there are variations on those themes by several other species of game bird, the most notable and popular of which is, no doubt, the pheasant.

———————•———————

The pheasant is not a native American bird. It is an Oriental and its behavior would be called by any good American pointing dog: inscrutable. But it is a favorite with hunters and with the painters of calendar art who love the big bird with the long tapered tail feathers and the gaudy green head. There must be thousands of paintings of pheasants breaking cover while two German shorthairs hold steady and the hunters are frozen in the act of mounting their guns.

It does happen that way. But it isn't something the experienced pheasant hunter expects.

The smart wild birds in the Plains states seem almost to know that they make big targets when they go out of the stubble of a cut-over grain field, trying hard to make it to the trees before the hunter gets off a shot. And for this reason, they don't fly readily. Instead, they run.

A pointing dog broken on other kinds of birds will have trouble with a pheasant. Just about the time he makes game and gets ready to go onto a point, the bird will start running ahead of him. The dog, exercising considerable restraint, will move up cautiously and, when he has the bird stopped again, go back onto a point. This is the time when the bird starts running again. So the dog has to move once

more and it is tempting, even for a well-trained dog, to rush the bird. This is especially true if the dog has seen the bird and, since the pheasant is a big bird, this is often the case.

Even if the dog can resist the temptation to rush on in, he will have to move fast, because a pheasant can move nimbly through the stalks and weeds of a cut-over field. Presumably, he is trying to reach the cover of a hedgerow or fence line before he flies and exposes himself. Whatever, he moves like he has a destination and is in a hurry to get there.

So the dog runs and, consequently, the hunters run after him. Because if the dog does crowd the bird and flush him, they want to be up there in good gun range. Running through the stubble at a high port, with one eye on the dog and the other on the ground in front of you, to spot any obstacles, is not the same thing as watching your dog from a distance, as you walk at a comfortable pace, gun over your shoulder or at your side. And then, since the dog will sometimes push a bird at extreme gun range, many hunters carry a twelve gauge for a little more power and reach. The gun can get heavy if you carry it long enough, especially if you are running and every muscle in your body is oxygen starved.

This is all by way of saying that pheasant hunting is not necessarily as easy as it looks. To the grouse hunter, it can look awfully easy. Too easy for some of them ever to give the sport a chance. A bird that big, flying in the clear, after a towering flush, just doesn't look like much of a challenge to them. But this, as noted, is not all that pheasant hunting is.

If you have good fields to hunt, flat and broken occasionally by fencerows or woodlots, and you are hunting pheasant with the right partner and the right dog—or dogs—then it is all the sport you could want. There is something about the size of that bird that inevitably startles you when it flushes, so that even the "easy" shots become a matter of some desperation. And the feeling of harvest is so keenly felt in pheasant hunting that it almost aches. You are generally on grain fields that have only recently been combined. The stalks are brown and sere. You feel the weather and you see the sky and the horizon so clearly that it seems almost possible to mark the degree to which it has gotten lower with the shortening of the days.

In a big recently combined corn field, you might use several hunters, half of them behind the dogs and half of them at a blocking position at one end of the field. It is close in tactics to the English driven shoots but, when you are in Iowa, a long way from them in spirit. Also, instead of using a dog that has been trained to staunch points and to hold steady to wing and shot, you may go for one of the flushing dogs or a retriever—a springer, say, or a Lab that will get on the scent of a bird and push it. The dog's job here is not to stand rock steady once he has made game but to make game and then close in, not at a rush but at a steady pace, almost like a dog trained to track men. The hunter knows right away when the dog is "birdy" and he can move on up, running if he has to, and be ready for the flush when it comes. With partners ready to block the end of the field, he knows that the bird will, sooner or later, have to fly and that someone will get a shot.

If you are lucky and know the country, you can hunt several fields this way during the course of a day. The walking will be relatively easy and, if your dogs work well and you shoot well, then you won't think of asking for anything more or comparing this hunting to anything else.

———————•———————

After the pheasant (there is no sense of a "ranking" at work here, sport is sport and it is the sportsman who either makes it into something profound or reduces it to something vulgar) you think of sharptail grouse and Hungarian partridge. Perhaps this is merely a geographic way of looking at things. The great pheasant hunting is in the Plains states. Iowa and the Dakotas have, by all accounts, the best pheasant hunting. Push farther west, into the region of the Continental Divide, and you are in the land of huns and sharpies.

The hun is a covey bird, twice the size, roughly, of the bobwhite.

But while it does invite comparison with the southern quail, there are important differences. Fot the shooter it comes down to this: the bobwhite lives in the thick broomweed and grass of the southeastern Piedmont while the hun lives in spare, cut-over western farmland. The first is very good for hiding so the birds stay put for protection; the other offers barely adequate concealment so the birds are quick to fly.

A dog that does well on huns might stop a full twenty yards from a covey of birds and go on point. And the birds might flush when you are still ten yards in back of the dog. So you have to shoot quick and shoot long; but if you can meet that challenge, you will have some fine demanding sport.

The sharptail is not a bird that is found in coveys. Not precisely, anyway. But it can be found in great numbers, especially in the vast, cut-over wheat fields of central Montana. Several hundred birds might be feeding in one large wheat field on a morning during the season. This can be too much action for some dogs—some hunters, too.

The birds will stand to a point, especially when they are in the islands of small trees and brush, called bluffs, around the big fields. Then the dog can work without the distractions of too many birds and too much shooting. The birds fly very much like a ruffed grouse but because they are larger than the ruff, hunters sometimes think they are slow, verging on ponderous in flight. It is a mistake that results in a lot of missed "easy shots."

Farther west is chukar country. These little partridges are real runners and the best dogs are those that can see the birds on the ground and then circle around and put the covey between dog and hunter. When the birds have been stopped this way, a hunter can get good shooting in reasonable range. They flush as coveys, much like huns and bobwhites.

The desert quail of the Southwest and the dry parts of California behave in much the same fashion and often the greatest and most frustrating challenge in hunting them is getting them to fly. They would much rather run and, truth be told, are probably as hard, or harder, to hit on the ground as in the air. A dog that can stop the birds by maneuvering to get them between himself and the hunter is a great asset.

Again, there is no ranking intended here. Nor is this brief list meant to be exhaustive. There are people who hunt the blue grouse in the higher elevations of the Rocky Mountain states and find him a fine game bird. Others feel the same way about the sage hen—though the literature of bird hunting is more concerned with the bobwhite, woodcock, ruffed grouse, and pheasant than with the other birds.

This is due in large part to the fact that, as hunting goes, the West is more a place for the big-game enthusiast than for the bird hunter. In the East, South, and Midwest, the opposite is true. In Alabama and Georgia, quail hunting is redolent with the kind of lore and ritual that attaches itself to elk hunting in Wyoming and Montana. The most serious hunters, including deer hunters, that you will find in New England, are the men who live all year for the three months of grouse season. And across Ohio, lower Michigan, Illinois, and on into Iowa and the Dakotas, pheasant hunters are in greater supply than places to hunt pheasant.

While the western states might rank birds below big game in the standing of sport, that doesn't mean the dedicated bird hunter has to go along. The fact that there are relatively few bird hunters in Montana leads, one hears, to the happy situation of uncrowded fields to hunt. One man I know says he finds the bird hunting in Montana absolutely as rewarding as the bird hunting he left in Vermont.

———•———

For years now, I've imagined a kind of grand tour of American bird hunting that would start out in the central plains of Montana in early September. For two weeks a small band (four or less) of happy hunters and their dogs would hunt the sharptails and huns, and then move east into South Dakota and Iowa for the pheasant. Once this began to wear a little thin and the cold winds down from Canada began to cut through the briar-proof clothes, they would push on to Minnesota, Wisconsin, and Michigan for grouse and woodcock, which they would stay with all the way into New England, admiring the rich changing of the leaves as they migrated east.

The last day of grouse season in Vermont (practical last day, not official) would be the opening day of deer season, so the hunters would make a long flanking movement south into Georgia, Alabama, or north Florida, where the quail season would just be starting. By now they would be into their third or fourth set of briar-proofs and the dogs would be gaunt with work. It might be time to add a strong pointer or two to the team in order to keep up the punishing pace.

By late February, dogs and hunters would be worn to exhaustion with ranging across the country, with the strain of anticipating the flush of every bird and every covey the dogs had pointed over the last five months. By the end of February they could all rest and think about next year when it would be time to do it all again. Maybe then, the men think, they'll make a couple of detours since it is a shame not to shoot some woodcock in Louisiana and some Gambel's quail in California, not to mention some chukars in Washington.

The sad fact of life is . . . there is never enough time for the truly important things.

8

Big Shoots

Dove

There is a form of hunting that almost everyone who likes to hunt birds will try sooner or later. It is not strictly upland bird shooting, since the hunters are not moving and dogs are used only to retrieve. In many ways, this kind of hunting—though it is thoroughly American in style and customs—puts you in mind of the driven shoots of England and the Continent. Many, many birds are shot at and quite a few killed. Shooters wait for the game to come flying past them. There are social events before and after the shoot, and a general festive atmosphere, often involving quite a few people.

This is dove shooting and it is high, energetic sport that will challenge the eyes of the very best shooter like nothing this side of long-range waterfowling. Dove fly fast and they juke in the air like Tony Dorsett putting a move on some baffled linebacker and leaving him tangled in his feet, watching his target glide on into the end zone. Dove shooting is easy and non-challenging as far as the hunting goes. You hardly walk at all and the only discomfort you will feel comes from the heat and the repetitious recoil as you shoot and shoot at those frustrating little birds.

Dove are legal game in about half the states. In others, there is fierce and frequent controversy over whether or not they should be designated game birds. Research has shown that in the states where the dove is classified as a songbird, its population is no healthier than in adjacent states where it is considered a game bird and hunted heavily.

This is not to enter the marshy terrain of arguments about hunting and wildlife populations and all the rest of it, but to make the point that dove are abundant and tough. They reproduce well in spite of the fact that, in some places, the survival rate of first-year birds is less than 20 percent. About 20 percent of the birds that are lost in that first year are killed by hunters and, in the states where there is no dove hunting, predators pick up the slack.

Dove migrate, so the seasons and bag limits in the various state jurisdictions are established within federal guidelines. Most states, especially in the Southeast where dove hunting is as popular as college football, split the season into two, or even three parts. In the earliest of the seasons,which starts when it is still technically summer and the heat lies on the land like a heavy tarp, shooters are taking mostly resident birds. Later, as the migratory birds come in, there will be a mix. The splitting of the seasons also allows both hunters and doves to settle down and rest their nerves periodically. In a heavily hunted area, there will be a lot of dove that have been shot at a dozen times or more and they can put on the afterburner and climb like a Phantom in a dogfight when they see yet another gunner. For their part, the shooters get a little jerky and quick after a couple of weeks of the season, shooting two or three boxes of shells at birds that can sometimes come whistling by at better than sixty miles an hour so that a sustained lead of twenty feet merely cuts a few tail feathers.

Dove generally go from their roosts to a grain field in the very early morning, then back to the roost, and then back to the grain once again in midafternoon. After the second feeding period, they will go somewhere for water and then, as evening begins to fall and their cooing seems so appropriate to the mood of the day, they will go back to the roost.

The predictability of a dove's schedule is of great benefit to the shooter, especially if he wants to make a social thing of the dove shoot. He can invite his guests and tell them exactly what time shooting will begin. It is all very settled and formal—which, again, makes the taking of dove more what would properly be called a "shoot" than a "hunt."

The first requirement is a field or a water hole ("tank" in Texas) to be shot. Dove will eat most grains but they love some things above all others. Browntop millet is a favorite food. Also sunflowers. But they will eat corn and soybeans and wheat and even, in my experience, pine mast and other wild seeds. But they will come into a millet field or a sunflower patch with real determination and in large numbers and this is what you want on a good dove shoot. The point here is not, as in grouse hunting, say, isolated moments of beautiful and almost choreographed action scattered through a long rhythmic day of walking and watching and waiting for something to happen. In dove hunting, what is desired is furious, almost hectic, action. And the first and central requirement for this is a good field with lots of food.

A word here about baiting. The law forbids the putting out of food to attract birds. The food must have grown on the ground that it covers. Every year, the local papers across the South are full of stories about citizens—some of them quite prominent—arrested for shooting over "baited fields." Sometimes, of course, it is simply a clear-cut violation of the law and sometimes, I think, genuine misunderstanding of what the law says. A man I know in south Alabama hunts dove righteously every September over a field that he has planted in millet. He goes through and rough-combines lanes into the field and leaves about half the millet standing and a lot of seed on the ground. Then he goes into town and finds the game warden and invites him to come out to his farm and look over the field he plans to hunt to make sure that everything is absolutely legal. The man once got clearance from one game warden and then, in the middle of the shoot, was checked by another who accused him of hunting a

baited field. The confusion was eventually cleared up and the shoot went on. But the episode does point up a degree of uncertainty that exists.

Once the field has been chosen and the shooters have been notified, there isn't much to do except hope for weather. Dove-shooting weather is clear and warm without too much wind. It isn't that dove won't fly on a windy day—rather, with a good tail wind, they'll fly faster than a lot of shooters find possible to believe, or make allowance for.

The shooter goes into the field with only himself and his gun and his retrieving dog and, possibly, a little folding chair to sit on. He will wear dark or muted clothing, perhaps camouflage if the birds have been shot at a lot already. Lightweight footgear. Glasses. He will carry a lot of shells. A mere two boxes (fifty shells) would indicate either a very confident or very parsimonious shooter. The limit varies year to year but twelve is a good average. The shooter who gets his limit on two boxes is killing almost one of every four birds he shoots at. Almost any dove shooter would be proud of a percentage like that.

The retriever can be a great help on a dove field, especially if the crop has not been close cut. The birds are a grey and dusty color with a slight creamy rose tinge to their breast feathers and when they fall into leaves and stalks of dried corn they can blend in perfectly. You don't want to spend a lot of time looking for a bird that you know you knocked down while thirty or forty more are angling overhead within easy gun range. The dog can retrieve while you keep shooting. And he can find birds a lot more efficiently then you can.

One word of caution: if you take a dog into a big dove field in the early part of the season, take some water along and be careful not to let the dog get too excited with all the action. Young and incompletely trained dogs may get too excited with all the shooting and either try to retrieve every bird they see fall or simply start running. Even a well-trained dog may run himself very hard just finding and retrieving your birds. A dog cannot shed heat efficiently and it is not uncommon for dogs to become incapacitated and die from heat stroke. The dog needs water to stay cool and, if it does work hard enough to get heat stroke, then immediate first aid is to cool the dog by immersing him completely in water.

The dove shooter may want a little more gun than the one he uses for quail—especially if he is shooting a big field where the birds have been shot at before. The ranges will tend to be long and dove can, as they say, take some killing. Still, many very good dove shooters us the same gun they use for quail but with a little more powder and slightly larger shot. In the end, of the millions and millions of shots fired at dove that are misses, only a tiny percentage are the fault of the gun.

———————— • ————————

A good dove shoot can be one man standing by a small pond in the evening, waiting for the birds to come to water. It can be half a dozen men who leave the office a little early and meet at a fifteen-acre cut-over corn field a few miles outside of town. Or it can be a full-blown affair with a big picnic lunch followed by a pig picking and oyster roast with live music, whiskey drinking and social dancing. In some parts of the South, a dove shoot is every bit as much of an event as the driven shoots were in Edwardian England. I remember having to turn down, reluctantly, an invitation to a dove shoot that would involve some five hundred shooters on thirty different fields. But that was just the beginning. After the shoot, there would be a huge barbecue followed by an outdoor concert and dance with music provided by none other than Merle Haggard. Somewhere in there, some bass fishing was also mentioned.

On some of these shoots the party becomes the main event and the bird shoot is more a prelude than anything else. For my taste, the best dove shoots involve a dozen or so shooters, all or most of whom know each other and might even have been shooting together for several years. I remember being invited on one of these when I had just gotten out of the service and had been away from home for several years. Nothing else could have made me feel quite so keenly that I was home as being invited on that hunt and going into a closet to inventory my hunting clothes and check the condition of my shotgun, which had been packed away in oil for the years I'd spent using other weapons.

I knew about half the men on the hunt that day. They were a lot like the men I'd said goodbye to a few days earlier—friendly men who did their jobs and spent a lot of time thinking about other things, like hunting or fishing. There were a couple of foresters among them and a lumberman or two. Parole officer. Farmer. Dentist. Country lawyer. I was made to feel like I fit right in.

"Sure does beat drilling around on some North Carolina parade ground, don't it?"

"That's a fact."

"Course I'd say a good afternoon dove shoot beat *almost* anything."

"Don't listen to him. Dove shooting is about the only thing he does. Sure don't do any work that anybody noticed."

"That's envy talking, son. Don't listen to it. Makes an ugly sound. Now, in honor of your making it home, we're going to give you the stand up the end of the field where they normally come in."

"That way you can show us how it's done."

"Or . . . we can learn from your mistakes."

"Try to let one or two get by so the rest of us can have some shooting."

"Hail, let him shoot 'em all. He's the one just came home."

"That's right. You just go on and shoot 'em all then. We'll watch and we'll help you pluck the birds later."

After some more of the same, we all began putting on our shooting vests and breaking open boxes of shells, dumping them into the vest pockets. Somebody passed around a thermos of iced tea and everyone had a drink.

"Hot. Whew *boy* it's hot."

"That's good. Those birds will be flying."

"But in this heat I'll be too wore out to shoot."

"You checking out your excuses already, are you?"

"What's yours?"

"I like 'The sun was in my eyes.' "

"Man, you have used that one *up*."

I followed the man who owned the field out a lane cut through the browntop, maybe a half mile to a fence where the field bordered a pasture full of Angus cattle. Just beyond the pasture, there was a large stand of mature planted pines.

"Lot of these birds will be coming from over there," he said, pointing in the direction of the pine trees. "Course, they'll be coming from all over, once it starts. But you'll get plenty of shooting right here."

"Thanks," I said.

"Welcome home."

A few minutes later a small flock of perhaps ten birds came over the cow pasture in my direction. They flew with the unmistakable darting and flaring and hesitating flight that makes dove so easy to identify and so hard to hit. I went down on one knee and tried to ease into the heavy growth along the fencerow. The birds were boring in straight for me. Just before they passed overhead I stood, mounted the gun, and fired at the first bird of the flock. I knew it was a good shot but I wasn't prepared for two birds to fall. I shot again as the birds were directly overhead and another crumpled. I fired my last shot (I was using a repeater) as the flock was going away and flaring from the noise of my gun. A fourth bird went down.

I couldn't believe it. And neither could anyone else on the field.

"Would you look at *that!*" someone shouted.

"Man should of stayed in the army. We *need* men who can shoot like that."

"Damn. If I'd known we were putting a hustler in the field, I'd have left this old heavy gun back in the car. No sense toting the thing if you can't shoot it."

"Look out, soldier, here comes another bunch."

Oh, but I was confident. Sure that all I'd needed was a little time away. All the mental circuitry was right now and I was a natural dove shooter. I couldn't miss. I started imagining myself getting a limit with less than ten shells. I'd be a legend.

The next pod of birds was boring in over the cow pasture and I waited supremely certain that I would do unto them what I had done unto the others. When they came in range, I rose into my lethal shooting posture, mounted my gun, and fired three times . . . without cutting a feather.

"Flew right through the pattern," one man shouted. "They'll do that to you."

"Hot *damned*," another said. "He's mortal."

For the next two hours, I proved it. Even with my brilliantly lucky start, I was still not high gun. Not even close. Like I said, there were some men on that field who lived to dove hunt and did not take it lightly. But they missed too—only not as often.

The birds came from every direction and every angle. They came by full bore, so fast that they blurred as you tried to lead them. And then they would sometimes drift by just as stately as a hunting hawk so that it was all you could do to keep the barrel moving. They came in high and they came in so low that you couldn't shoot because you might scatter the shooter in the next stand. They made every kind of fool of me that it is possible to make of a man without driving him completely from the field. I loved every minute.

The other men did, too. And when somebody made a good shot and the others weren't too busy to notice, a cheer of approval would come up from the men around the field. And when somebody missed a lagging, low-flying bird with three straight shots, somebody would inevitably holler, "Man, that bird is *strong*. Got to be to take three full loads of number eights and keep on flying like that."

Two hours after it started, the action slowed. Then died. Men began to walk slowly back through the field to the shade of the live oak where we had parked the cars. Dogs followed some of the men, moving as wearily as their masters. The sun was lower now, not quite to the tree line, and the fragrance of pine was on the air, the way it is at night. Off in the distance, a few wood ducks were circling a small juniper swamp. There was a moon the shape of a perfect fingernail pairing hanging low in the still blue sky.

"Well, how'd you do?" a man asked me.

"About as well as I did the last time I tried this."

"That's good. Least you didn't get no worse. I got nine. Shot two boxes plus what I had loose in my vest. Missed shots so easy I believe one of those cows could have made them. I just don't believe I'll ever get to be a good dove shooter."

"Me either."

"But I don't plan to quit trying."

"Me either."

Somebody had a big fiberglass cooler full of beer and ice in the bed of his pickup. He passed the beer around and we all drank gratefully and listened to ourselves complain and exaggerate, which are the two acceptable modes of after-hunt discourse. One man had missed a shot so easy that the only thing easier would have been to take a lead on the ground itself and shoot it. Another said he didn't see *how* a little old bird like that could fly that fast without burning his blamed feathers up.

Nobody was bragging.

Pretty soon somebody said, apologetically, that he'd better be getting home since his wife would be holding supper. Then another man said he reckoned he might as well get on, too. The cars and trucks filled up and the goodbyes were said and everybody said that next week, by damned, they were going to come back to this field and really powder them.

One of the last men to leave, the one who owned the field, said to me, as he was getting in his pickup, "Thanks for coming."

I nodded and said, "I wouldn't have taken anything for it."

And that was the God's truth.

9

Mighty Tom

Turkey

Turkey hunting—especially spring turkey hunting—is nothing less than a fine madness. It isn't upland bird hunting in the strictest sense, but then it isn't like anything else in all of sport either, so there is no categorizing it. Turkey hunting is something wholly unto itself.

As everyone knows, the wild turkey was Benjamin Franklin's choice as the nation's symbol. He preferred it to the bald eagle because the turkey seemed to embody those virtues he thought made for a happy personal and national life. Turkeys were smart and sociable, surviving on wit and work while the eagle, which eventually got the job of national bird, was a solitary, aggressive raptor, a beautiful bully.

Anyone who has hunted turkeys will at least share Franklin's regard for their intelligence. It is hard to credit a mere bird with so much cunning but after a few demonstrations you will be thoroughly convinced. Fred Bear, the master bow hunter, says that of all the game in the world, the hardest to hunt is the white-tailed deer. Then he says that the only thing that keeps the turkey from being that hard is that it lacks a sense of smell. Otherwise, he says, its instinctive caution and its remarkable eyesight and hearing make it a very difficult kill.

The undeniable challenge of getting into shotgun range of a gobbling turkey is a big part of the hold it has on people who are half mad for the sport. The other part is in the season and the technique, both of which are unique in hunting and about as seductive as anything I know.

Turkeys mate in the spring. Hens and gobblers are split up then and they are trying to find each other, urged on by their biology. They find each other by calling and it is the call of the turkey that the hunter must master. Gobblers, of course, gobble. But that is not the important call from the hunter's point of view, though it can be useful. The hunter must know how to imitate the hen, to attract the gobbler.

Calling turkeys is something you learn with practice. There are all sorts of commercially made turkey calls. And a few oldtimers use some that they make from the wing bone of a hen turkey. Among the manufactured types, the diaphragm and the slate and the box are the most popular. The slate and the box both use friction and are worked with the hands. You can pick one up and be making noises that sound something like a turkey within a few minutes. A few hours of practice will make you good enough to go into the woods. The best way to practice is to listen to an instructional tape and then try to make your call sound like what you are hearing on the tape. You can record your own calls and compare them to those on the tape.

The diaphragm call is preferred by a number of hunters because you do not need your hands to work it. They believe—with very good reason—that any movement whatsoever when you are calling a gobbling turkey is likely to alert the bird before he gets in good gun range. The diaphragm call is merely a piece of thin Latex stretched tight around a frame that fits into the roof of the hunter's mouth. He can close this off and use it as a reed, blowing air past it and vibrating it to make a sound . . . which will resemble the notes of a hen turkey, with practice.

Learning to use a diaphragm does take some time. When you

first fit one into your mouth, your reflex is to gag. Then, once you have gotten accustomed to having the thing in there, you still can't get it to make any noise when you blow against it. When I first tried to learn I had just about decided that I would never get the damned thing to work; then one day, I got it to make a pitiful *squak*. That was all the encouragement I needed and for the next two or three days, I had the call in my mouth everywhere I went. I practiced especially hard when I was in the car. Hands busy, just like when I'd be hunting, but nothing for my mouth to do.

It was spring, in Alabama, and warm. I was driving around with the windows of my car rolled down, blowing through that diaphragm for all I was worth and I was starting to get some pretty sweet notes to come through it. I was stopped at a light in town, thinking about a big strutting gobbler and blowing a few sweet hen-in-heat notes on that diaphragm when I felt eyes. I looked to my left and there was a car pulled up next to mine. The driver was a middle-aged woman, dressed for some banking and then lunch, and she was looking at me like she couldn't quite make up her mind whether or not to find a phone and call the cops. I tried to smile but I don't think it warmed her up much. I can imagine her going home to her husband that night and telling him about this strange man she'd seen stopped at a light in town.

"What was so strange about him, dear?" he would say, no doubt thinking that she had seen some long-haired fellow with an earring and a tattoo.

"Well, he *looked* all right, you know. Clean and dressed well. And he was driving a nice car."

"Well, what was it then?"

"Well, he was . . . ah, he was making these *noises*."

"What sort of noises?"

"That's just it. They weren't human noises. I know that. They sounded almost like *turkeys*, if you can believe that."

"Turkeys?"

"Yes. Turkeys. He was working very hard on those noises, too. He didn't even notice me at first. Just sat there staring at the light and making turkey noises, looking very pleased with himself."

"Turkey noises," the husband would say, mulling it over, "right in the middle of town?"

"Yes. And the thing of it was, they were very *good* turkey noises. He wasn't just doing child sounds. He'd been *working* on those turkey noises."

"Well," the husband would say soothingly, "I don't know what to make of it. But I suppose it does prove that there are all kinds of nuts out there."

A turkey hunter will be called a nut, or worse, many many times in his life. His best friends, and his family, will say those hard words to his face. So he might as well learn early to accept that sort of misunderstood criticism and a little public practice with a diaphragm call is a good way to get started.

Also, it is an essential if you are ever going to kill a bird. Because you cannot sneak up on a gobbler. If you are moving, he will see you and move out. The tactical problem of turkey hunting always starts with the hunter in a stationary position and the gobbler on the move. The hunter then brings the gobbler into range by calling. The call sounds like that of a hen. So if you are going to hunt turkeys, the first thing you must do is get a call and learn how to use it well. Learn the various hen sounds—yelps, cackles, purrs, and clucks—and how to put them together at least convincingly and, if possible, seductively. Make yourself sound like a coquettish hen turkey and forget about what your friends say.

Once you have mastered the call, then you need to find some turkeys. Scouting is important, even crucial, because when the time comes, you want to go directly to a spot where you will have a good chance of calling a bird. The more time you spend wandering around the woods, the better your chances of alarming any birds that might be there.

The first step in a scouting operation is to find a likely roosting area. Turkeys like fairly big and open woods and they roost in tall, ladder-limbed trees which are often—but not necessarily—mature conifers. They eat acorns and various nuts and seeds and mast so if you know of a large stand of tall nut-bearing hardwoods that are fairly clear of ground cover and have a small adjacent stand of big old pines, you might want to start checking it out a couple of weeks before the season starts.

The best way to determine if there are turkeys in this area is to go out at first and last light and try to roost one by using a locator call. For some reason a turkey on the roost will almost always gobble back at certain noises. An owl will almost always get a turkey started. A crow sometimes will. Another gobbler sometimes works.

So at the proper hour, which is dawn or dusk, you slip into the woods and get about four hundred yards from the area you think might be holding roosting birds and you make a few hoots like an owl. (You can buy a call or a tape which will teach you how to make the sound with your own mouth. As long as you are going to be thought a fool for talking like a turkey, you might as well start hooting like an owl, too.)

If you hear a gobble in response, then you have found the place to hunt. Mark it and leave the woods and keep it to yourself.

When the day comes, you go back to that spot a quarter of an hour or so before first light. Do not try to get much closer than two hundred yards from a roosting turkey; if you spook the bird before dawn you are finished with him for the day. Find a large tree with a fairly clear area out in front for forty yards. Make sure that you are dressed in camouflage and that your face is either painted in camouflage paint or covered with a camouflage net. Wear camouflage gloves and you might even want to wrap your gun in some camouflage tape. Keep your gear to a minimum since you don't want to be carrying anything that might make a sudden, startling noise.

Sit with your back to the large tree and hold your gun in some comfortable fashion so that you can mount it cleanly and quickly when the time comes. Relax, settle down, wait a few minutes and, when the first light begins to bleed in between the trees, start calling.

There are several schools of thought (what else?) on just how much calling is good at this point in the game. One of the best turkey hunters I know makes a single soft cluck and then stays off the call for as long as an hour, or until he is sure that the gobbler is not coming to the sound. Another good hunter I know starts out with a tree call—a series of soft yelps. His ideas is that the hen turkeys are sort of talking themselves awake at this time of morning and he wants to imitate that. I've heard more good turkey hunters say you can call too much and too loud than the other way around. It seems logical that a new hunter, especially, would want to be restrained in his calling since he probably hasn't mastered the call yet and might give himself away if he stays on it too long. Too much calling will keep a turkey on the roost, waiting for the hen to walk into his landing area. Once the gobbler is on the ground you should yelp about every fourth time he gobbles.

Sometimes the gobbler will answer that first call from the roost and then the game is really on. It is difficult for someone who has never been there to understand just what a bone-deep thrill it is to hear a gobbler answer your call. The sound is more powerful and urgent than anything you could imagine a mere bird could make. And you know after you've heard it that, from now on, it is strictly a match of wits. You cannot use anything except your skill at calling and concealment. You must wait the bird out and the excitement in that is one of those exquisite, escalating sensations that leave you with a dry mouth, trembling hands, and a fluttering heart.

The bird decides that those soft clucks and yelps could only be made by a hen turkey and he makes up his mind to claim her. He flies down off the roost, to a spot some one hundred and fifty yards from where you are sitting. When he hits the ground, he gobbles. You wait a while and then, when he gobbles again, a little closer, you answer with a few soft notes.

He gobbles again.

All right.

A few minutes later, he gobbles again. You respond with something soft and enticing. He booms something back. Male vanity is at work here; he wants the hen to come to him. But if it comes right down to it . . . well, he'll give in. So you wait and blow a few more soft notes that are answered by another booming gobble and then . . . you see the turkey.

He comes walking in, massive chest pumped out, head erect and alert, legs moving in a comic strut. When he is out in the middle of your clearing and your ears are roaring with the tension, he spreads his tail feathers, drops his wings, and cuts loose. The gobble raises the decible count in your ears to something nearly unbearable.

For a minute or two, you watch the big bird strut and gobble for the hen he imagines is watching. When the turkey turns his back to you and his head is behind the fanned tail feathers, or steps behind a tree, you smoothly raise your gun and sight down the barrel. When he turns again, you aim at the head which is normally blue and white but now shows more red where it is gorged with blood . . . and you shoot.

It can happen that way. That is more or less the ideal, the turkey hunt as scripted by the hunter. But there are a thousand ways it can go wrong and you may spend a morning where you heard birds gobbling the previous evening, and never hear a note. Sometimes, because of changes in the weather or the moon or for reasons beyond the ability of humans to penetrate, the turkeys will just stop gobbling for a morning or two.

Or you could spend a long morning gobbling to a turkey that is already servicing a group of hens. He is not willing to leave them for just one more. Another turkey may come along and claim them. But he will gobble long and loud to proclaim the availability of his wonderful self, hoping the hen will decide to come to him. A lot of hunters will try, after an hour or two of this, to sneak in on the gobbling turkey. It is a futile exercise. The gobbler will shut down and move off.

Sometimes, in a case like this, a hunter can force the gobbler to show himself by imitating the sound of another gobbler. Then the bird that has been answering the hunter's hen calls will think his territory is being invaded and he will come out to fight the rival that he imagines has come to challenge him. When this happens, the bird will come on the hunter in a rush, ready for combat.

Veteran turkey hunters will warn you against trying to call a gobbling turkey downhill or across water. "They don't like to get their feet wet, Jeff," a very good turkey hunter in Alabama once told me, to account for why I'd spent a morning on one side of a little juniper-choked draw calling to a gobbler who answered my every note but would not move one foot closer to me no matter how much urgency I put into the call.

But, since they are wild creatures, they will often do what they are not supposed to do. And even when they do what they are supposed to do, they will do it with such caution that you may not get a shot or the bird will see you just as you begin to mount the gun and start moving out with a nervous *put put put* and you will try to shoot him on the run or in flight, which lowers the odds considerably. A turkey takes a lot of killing and almost all hunters use high-based or magnum loads and big shot—number fours being commonplace. Some gunners will use a twenty gauge but most want the extra fire-power of a twelve. You aim for the head because a body shot often cripples a bird that you will never retrieve. A head shot will be fatal even if only one pellet in the pattern strikes. Most turkey hunters like a tight-choked gun since many shots will be long and . . . there will not be many opportunities in even the best turkey hunter's life-time so he will want to take advantage of them all. Within reason, of course.

All of the turkey's stealth and majesty go into making it the sport that it is. The kind that will have a man getting up three hours earlier than usual for four weeks running to go out into the woods when it is still dark and make a lot of strange noises, hoping to fool an unseen bird out there in the trees and gloom. Game that magnificent demands a level of commitment that borders on the obsessive and most turkey hunters willing make that commitment. You can spot them midseason by the red eyes that are sunken into the sockets like pebbles settled into a bed of clay. And by the way they talk incessantly about how they've got a "bird that's been talking every morning for a week now but just won't come in. But tomorrow . . . maybe tomorrow."

The other element that makes turkey hunting more an addiction or a righteous calling than a simple pastime is that it is done in the spring of the year when the land is coming back and the other birds are making their own mating calls, filling the woods with the sweet music of renewal. The leaves are coming out and if you hunt the Southeast, the shady green will be shot through with the chaste white petals of blooming dogwood. Redbud will be blooming too and the scent of wysteria will be on the air. It will have been some time since you hunted anything and the pleasure you feel at being once again out in the woods will be almost unbearably keen even if you do not find a big noisy, crafty gobbler to match wits and calls with. It is a time of glory. It is a good time to go a little mad.

———•———

You can also hunt turkeys in the fall. Then it is a different game. You look for the large flocks of birds since that is how they travel at that time of year. When you do find one, you scatter the flock and sit on the ground and wait. After a few minutes, you begin calling. The notes you use under these conditions are not the same ones you use in the spring of the year. Now you call *kee kee kee*. This is the whistle-like sound the young turkeys make to regather the flock. Eventually the birds will begin coming back to the point where they were dispersed. You will be waiting, camouflaged, for them to come into gun range.

Most states that have a fall season allow the killing of birds of either sex. In the spring, only the gobblers are legal game. Gobblers are distinguished by their beards, which are wiry strands of hair that grow from the breast and reach nine inches or more in length on the mature gobblers. In the spring, many hunters will pass up young males of the year, called "jakes," which can be distinguished by the short length—two or three inches—of beard. Jakes often travel together and will fill the woods with their calling. But for all the noise they are harder to bring in than a mature gobbler. Sometimes a jake will run point security for an older bird so that a hunter will be confronted with two strutting turkeys, a smaller bird in close and the big boy just a little farther out. This is the sort of thing that turkey hunters dream of in their delirium.

Some fall hunters have begun to experiment with dogs—hound and setter crosses—which will help the hunter locate and scatter the flocks and will then sit immobile inside a hastily built blind of camouflage netting while the hunter calls the birds in. These dogs could be a tremendous help in finding traveling flocks of birds in the big woods.

Fall turkey hunting is a fine departure for the hunter who has been working the same bird coverts for days and days and is ready for a change of pace. It gets him into different country and challenges his skill at reading the woods and the signs of the game he is hunting. But it is not the same thing as the spring hunting. Nothing is.

10

The Guns

If you are going to hunt birds, then you are going to have to carry a shotgun. That is an inflexible rule and there is no getting around it. Presumably, this means you will have to own a shotgun (no one rents them as far as I know and borrowing from a friend isn't good form) and when you get around to buying a shotgun, it is much harder. Because there simply are no rules.

Well, very few at any rate. You will not want to hunt birds with a ten gauge that has thirty-six-inch barrels, for example. But once you get past a few obvious strictures, you are on your own, flying blind.

Books will not be much help. One very well-known sportsman, Frank Woolner, writes in his *Grouse and Grouse Hunting* that he likes to hunt grouse with a twelve-gauge automatic, a Winchester made with glass barrels. Another sportsman, Nick Sisley, writes in his *Grouse and Woodcock* that his favorite grouse gun is a twenty-gauge Italian-made automatic. If you went only on the advice of these two writers, both of whom have excellent credentials, you would logically conclude that you want either a twenty or a twelve gauge, in either a domestic or imported model. Only one thing would seem solidly established—your gun must be an autoloader.

Well, if you read another ten books, nine of them would insist that the pure bird-hunting gun, the Platonic distillation of all its essences, would be a short-barreled side-by-side double. The tenth book would agree that the double is the correct gun for upland birds but that the barrels should be stacked. Somewhere, no doubt, there is a book that sings the praises of the old-fashioned pump gun for birds, but I haven't found it.

The proper way to look at this is to consider it a blessing. If there isn't any tight orthodoxy about guns for upland birds, then you are liberated in advance. Free to follow your own tastes and eccentricities and shoot the gun that is absolutely right for you.

Now there are all sorts of considerations that you will have to factor into your decision about buying a gun or guns. One of the first is whether to go with a custom gun or get something off the rack.

A custom gun is not absolutely necessary for everyone. But for some people it is a great help. Just as people with non-typical builds need to have their clothes custom made, so the fitted gun is crucial for people who are much larger or smaller than average.

A gun that is fitted to you will have the right length through the stock, the right drop, and the correct degree of cast, so that when you mount the gun everything is where it should be and you will hit what you are looking at. If you have long arms, the stock will be a little longer than the standard fourteen inches. If you have a long neck and have to bend it excessively to get your face over the barrels, then a little extra drop can be added to the stock to compensate. Since your eye is the rear sight of a shotgun, it must be aligned with the center of the rear of the receiver, up the center of the rib through the front sight. In order to compensate for different facial configurations, cast can be put into the stock.

All this fitting is best done with a try gun, which is a gun that has a stock that is adjustable by means of screws. The smith can make adjustments in the stock as you mount the gun until he has exactly the right dimensions for you; these go into the stock when the gun is built. If a fitting with a try gun is not possible, then you can send your body measurements to the gunmaker and he can work very closely, using them.

A fitted gun, of course, will not automatically make you into a good shot. That takes hard work, practice, good instruction. But the custom gun can be a help and there is a good feeling that comes along with knowing that you have exactly the right tool and that it was made just for you. It is hard to think of anything for which a man feels more pride of ownership than a gun. To know that the gun has been carefully made to his specifications only adds to this feeling.

The great classic custom guns are side-by-side doubles. And there is a lot to be said for them. Many hunters consider their appearance to be the shotgunning equivalent of the Mercedes's shape. Also, there are shooters who claim that the wide plain of the twin barrels gives you more of a sighting surface. This is especially so if you are keeping the blurred image of the gun barrels—as well as the bird—in your field of view. Finally, there is the fact that the side-by-side double with twin triggers is, as firearms go, a very simple and dependable piece. It can fire thousands of rounds without any easing of the fine tolerances to which it has been built. Outside of the lock, which is only five moving parts, little moves and there is only a small amount of friction. This lack of complicated machinery enables the gun maker to shave weight so a good double in a twenty gauge can weigh as little as five pounds and still be perfectly balanced and solid to the shoulder. The gun is also safer than a repeater since it can be easily unloaded for crossing fences or when the gun is handed to another shooter.

When you come right down to it, the side-by-side double is a very hard gun for the upland bird hunter to improve upon. Which makes a kind of sense in that the gun itself has not been improved upon since roughly the turn of the century when the visible hammer guns gave way to those with hammers concealed inside the action. Since then, there have been no significant improvements.

So with the engineering opportunities exhausted, pure craft came to the fore. With the possible exception of the split-cane fly rod, there is nothing in sport so redolent of fine, loving craftsmanship as the well-made side-by-side gun. Before the Second World War and the final, definitive end of the apprentice system, there were several quality gun makers in England. They probably made a few thousand guns every year. A few years ago, when Leigh Perkins searched England for a maker to supply him with quality side-by-side doubles, he found that there are only four hundred guns made there every year. And the prospects are dim for the half dozen remaining makers.

The finest is James Purdey and Sons—though many knowledgeable people prefer the Boss guns to Purdeys. People who don't otherwise know very much about sport know about the Purdey gun, which is routinely written up in sporting and non-sporting magazines as the "Rolls Royce of shotguns" and is collected by some people who have no intention of shooting them. One Hollywood director has it written into his contracts that as part of his fee he is to be presented with a Purdey.

You can still go to Purdey's on South Audley Street and for $15,000 order a gun made to fit only you. Expect two years or more from fitting to delivery. The company makes seventy-five guns a year. In one hundred and seventy years of business, they have made not quite thirty thousand.

The Holland and Holland Company also still makes guns, for slightly less. And so do a few other London establishments. And once you leave England there are gunmakers across Europe, especially in Spain and Italy. Orvis uses both Italian and Spanish makers to make the custom guns it sells. The Italians and the Spanish gunmakers make a light fast gun that is a real pleasure to handle and to look at. If their guns are not up to those of the English in particular matters these are the quality of the engraving and the final polished luster of the wood.

So the carefully made gun, assembled under the supervision of one experienced craftsman, is not extinct, though it is no longer available in the numbers it once was. And no comeback is likely. However, the good news is that since these guns last virtually forever, there are plenty of them available in the second market. You can buy a good Boss or Webley & Scott through several sources, among them the tradepaper *American Shotgunner* or through *The Orvis News*, the company's newsprint bi-monthly.

Not all the good old guns are English. There are some American classics, especially the Parker and the Winchester Model 21. Thousands of Parkers in a number of grades were built before the company was folded into Remington Arms some fifty years ago. There are Parker aficionados who are every bit as passionate about the object of their desires as Purdey lovers are about theirs. The Parker is a much more American gun. Most are heavier and sturdier and, therefore, not as quick to mount . . . or to break. Americans tend, as mentioned before, to take their guns out hunting. The English, on the other hand, find a nice comfortable butt somewhere and shoot what is driven toward them. For a lot of American bird hunters, what these Parkers lose in quickness is more than made up for by what they gain in toughness. But here, as in all matters relating to shotguns, the decision is personal. As far as value goes, the fine Parkers are valued as much as any English gun. I saw one auctioned at Christie's in New York for $95,000.

Another American classic side-by-side is the Winchester 21, which started out as something close to a factory gun and quickly achieved the status of nobility. The Model 21 was a very good production gun, built to be indestructible, and then a better custom gun, though it never matched the British guns, which even the most patriotic American shooter will admit, set a standard not likely to be matched.

In buying a Parker or a Winchester Model 21 or any other gun of quality it is important to get good advice. The money spent on an appraisal can be money you will be glad you spent. Especially if the Model 21, for instance, that is being offered as a pigeon-grade custommade turns out to be nothing more than a production gun. There are people in the business of making appraisals and you can even send a piece to them—you pay for insurance and shipping as well as a fee for the appraisal—if you are somewhere too remote to do your business in person.

The love of shotguns—of fine old doubles, especially—can quickly become a passion every bit as compelling as the hunting of birds. It is a commonplace that things are not so well made today as they once were. And it is not always certain the people who make that complaint would like to go back to the good old days.

One interesting aspect to this whole matter of fine old guns as opposed to the inferior stuff that we see on the market today: it is not entirely a question of supply. If there were enough hunters out there willing to pay the price for a fine new double gun, then in time the industry it took to supply them might come back. There are all sorts of cottage crafts that have been through a recent renaissance; people are once again making things by hand to fill a demand. But the fact is, a man with $15,000 to spend on a shotgun would probably *rather* spend it on a fine old gun than go to London and be fitted for a new Purdey. The demand is not there. And this, I think, is mildly tragic. The great old gunmakers did such good work that they have, in a way, made it impossible for their own tradition to survive. All this is by way of pointing up something that often gets missed and to say, once again, that sportsmen are some of the most fierce traditionalists in existence outside of the Church.

———————•———————

Let's say you don't want to shoot a side-by-side, classic or otherwise. It doesn't matter why you don't because, remember, that is entirely a matter of personal choice. Maybe some farmer once chased you out of his watermelon patch, shooting rock salt at you through the barrels of an old side-by-side and the experience has poisoned you forever. Whatever. You don't like side-by-sides but you still want to shoot. What's left?

Well, there is another double you can shoot. The over-and-under. Classicists do not like the look of the gun and will argue that it has aiming drawbacks. They will claim that because of the way the gun is stocked, it will tend to shoot high. They will say that it lacks the wide sighting plain that makes it easy for a shooter with a

side-by-side to get barrels and bird in a proper relationship and, also, to see if he is shooting with his barrels canted.

The advocates of over-and-unders will counter by saying that their guns can be designed so that the barrels impact at the same point. They will say also that the recoil forces of an over-and-under are relatively consistent, barrel to barrel, while the side-by-side has some torque and will go one way on one barrel and another on the other. And they point out that many more championship shooters at clay birds use an over-and-under when they go for a double gun.

One expert, interviewed by Bob Brister for his book *Shotgunning*, said that he favored side-by-sides when the shooting problem was largely a matter of tracking and over-and-unders when the problem was chiefly in the vertical.

So, once again, it comes down to personal choice. For whatever it is worth, I shoot a side-by-side and my wife shoots an over-and-under.

Is there any reason why you should stay with the double gun, in either side-by-side or over-and-under, instead of going with a re-peater?

Some experts say, "Yes. Several."

Probably the most convincing argument for carrying a double on a bird hunt is that each barrel can be choked differently. The choke of a gun barrel is in the last two inches where the diameter can be necked down or opened up. The effect is to keep the shot in a relatively tight pattern as it leaves the barrel and flies out toward the target or, alternatively, to allow it to spread. Longer ranges require tighter chokes—full and modified. Closer shots call for wider patterns and, thus, more open chokes—cylinder (no change in barrel shape) or improved cylinder (a slight necking of the barrel in the last two inches). With a gun that has only one barrel, you can only have one choke, unless you equip it with one of those variable choke devices which hunters call "birdcages" and which ruin the lines of your gun. You can buy spare barrels or barrels that allow you to screw choking devices into the last two inches. While this will enable you to change from a tightly choked gun for one hunt—on ducks, say—to a more open choked gun on another—bobwhite—and thus own only one gun for all your hunting, it is not practical to be fooling around in the field, changing from your open barrel to a tight one because a pheasant has just flushed at extreme range. With a two-triggered double, one barrel in full and one in modified, you can do this easily and routinely. Or, if you are buying your gun for, say bobwhite, and you know that virtually all your shots will be at close-flushing birds and that your second shot will be at those same birds—going away and, hence, a little farther out—you can get a double with a single trigger that fires the open-choked barrel first and the tighter choked barrel next. Wide pattern for the close shot, tighter when the range is increased. That, in my view, is a real advantage.

Another argument for the double is that it is shorter than either an automatic or pump. A double with twenty-six-inch barrels will be about three or four inches shorter than an automatic with the same barrel length. This is because the autoloader needs a receiver to accommodate the bolt and feeding machinery. Three inches can make quite a difference in a close and crowded grouse covert. Even with short barrels, the bird hunter will find himself swinging on target only to have the barrels blocked suddenly and quite finally by a tree limb.

Also, and equally important, the shorter gun is quicker on the mount and swings more easily through the same arc according to some principle of geometry that isn't as important to name as to know and once you have carried a little double on one trip and then a long and generally heavier autoloader on the next trip, you will appreciate the principle, even if you cannot remember its name.

But aren't there hunters who go after birds with autoloaders and pumps?

Yes. There are. Plenty of them. And they are just as firmly convinced that theirs is the correct logic as the double gunners are convinced that their path is the one true road to success in the field. One point that cannot be argued is that you can get more shots off with a repeater, since most of them are chambered for five rounds.

It is rare that the grouse hunter can actually benefit from even a third shell—though some of the old market gunners carried pump guns with five shells and could flush covied birds in the late summer or early fall and kill one with every shell. And there are those occasions, especially in the early part of the season, when you find grouse still in pairs or even clusters. It will happen that one bird will flush, you will take the shot, and then two more will get up. Rare as doubles on grouse are, there have been triples.

Quail hunters have a more legitimate need for that third (or fourth or even fifth) shot. On a close covey rise—especially if the birds come up in staggered fashion—a good man can get off as many well-aimed shots as his gun will hold. There are oldtimers who get three, four, and five birds on the covey rise. But, then, there are a lot of hunters who would say that this misses the point.

———•———

A word about gauge. This is again a matter of personal preference but there is a little more for the hunter to go on when choosing bore size. Small close birds requiring quick gun handling can be killed with light loads in small bores. Indeed, there is some very good data that indicates a twenty-eight-gauge gun will shoot just as "hard" as a twenty . . . or close enough that the difference is insignificant in the field. Many very accomplished bird hunters would make the argument that you increase the chances of clean kills by carrying a twenty-eight when you are hunting quail or grouse. For two reasons. First, the lighter gun will improve your handling and, second, it will reduce fatigue so that you won't be moving the gun lazily late in the day.

The important point here is that what you are looking for is clean killing. There is no hunting analogue to light lines and leaders in fishing. If you make a mistake and break off a fish that you have hooked on a light tippet, the fish is free; but if you hit a bird with too light a load, you may simply cripple him and cause him to suffer until he makes a meal for some fox. A cripple that cannot be recovered is one of the low moments in a day of hunting. It bothers any hunter worthy of the name to cripple a bird and many hunters take it so hard that it virtually ruins a day's hunting for them. If the cause is bad shooting, bad luck, or bad weather that makes it impossible for the dog to find scent, then it is just one of those things. The bad that you must be prepared to accept along with the good in this life. But if you are crippling birds because you are shooting light loads in a small-bore gun because you think it is somehow sportier and more challenging, then you need to rethink your choice and your definitions. Make sure your shot, bore, and pattern are correct for clean kills on the game you are hunting at the ranges you expect to be shooting.

———————•———————

Another last word. Modern powders and steels have made cleaning guns less than the mandatory end-of-the-day exercise it used to be. But it is still a good idea to keep some lubrication on metal surfaces, to swab out the barrels, and to keep the action clean with a brush and some kind of solvent. Most people who have been around guns for a while would have to be physically restrained from cleaning them. And so far there hasn't been anything developed to keep guns from rusting where they have gotten wet or where a sweaty palm has set up some corrosion.

Properly cleaned guns should also be properly stored and transported. A soft case is all right for the trunk of the car or the back seat, when you are doing the loading and unloading. But if you are going on an airplane, you should pack your guns in a hard, lockable case. And, needless to say, you should have them appraised and insured whether or not you travel with them. A good shotgun, properly cared for, should survive its owner and perhaps its next owner as well. Some of the fine old guns have been around for the equivalent of four generations now and there is nothing at all worn or broken down about them. There is something about that kind of durability that makes you almost as much a custodian of the piece as an owner. You have a kind of obligation (non-enforceable, which may make it stronger in some important way) to care for the piece and make sure that it is passed on in good condition. There is nothing frivolous or disposable and trendy or fashionable about a good-quality shotgun. It is serious piece of workmanship, meant to do a serious job properly. In that lies a large measure of its appeal.

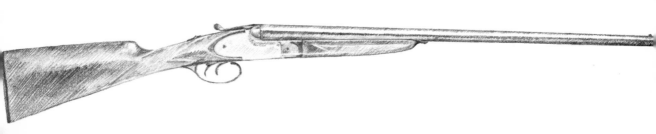

11

Pointers
on Pointers

It is unusual to find a hunter who likes hunting with dogs but is not passionate about it. Some men try hunting with bird dogs and, because they have badly trained or bred dogs, give it up in frustration. But nobody ever tries it and then gets enough of it after a while and drifts away from it. Going into the field with a dog soon becomes the only way of hunting for most people who try it. Many lose interest entirely in those kinds of hunting that do not involve a dog, finding them flawed and incomplete, like a ballet without music or a fine meal without wine. Without the dog, the exercise is flat and unappealing.

This is not merely a matter of numbers, either. There are places in this country where you can hunt birds without a dog and feel fairly confident that it won't cost you shots. This is especially true of ruffed grouse in New England and the Great Lakes states where some very capable hunters believe that even an able dog will flush more birds—or at least as many—out of range than he will point within it. And many of these walkup shooters kill enough birds that it doesn't pay to argue with them. However, it is relatively certain that they do not retrieve as many dead birds as hunters who use dogs do.

Even so, there are hunters who wouldn't walk birds up if you guaranteed them they would get more shooting that way. They would pass up the extra shots for the pleasure of hunting with the dog.

The feeling can be so strong that it defies rationality. One man I know, a fine bird hunter who once hunted every day, all day long, during the season, found himself unable to hunt when his dog got old. His dog was good and he'd been asked by a lot of other hunters who had females of the same breed if his dog would stand stud. He obliged but always took the fee, never the pick of the litter, I suppose because he couldn't stand the idea of an heir. He did this even as his own dog was growing first a little slow and then genuinely old, too old to hunt as vigorously as he once had, then too old to hunt all day and, finally, too old to hunt at all. Through all of this, the man could not bear to get another dog. He would hunt for a forlorn hour now and then with his own dog, or go out for the day once in a while with someone who had invited him out to hunt behind a young dog— often one that had been sired by the old dog. But he didn't put one tenth of the time in field that he once had, back in the days when his dog was young and strong.

The man plainly could not separate hunting from that dog. They'd had too many good days together in the field, over too many years, for him just to cast the dog off like rundown machinery.

Most bird hunters would understand that story.

———————•———————

The elementary explanation for why you hunt birds with a dog is simple enough. You find more birds that way. The dog has instincts that have been refined through centuries of breeding that enable him to smell the birds. There are techniques, also, that have been developed over the same centuries that enable a man to control the dog and to make him do something he really does not want to do—namely, stand on a steady point when he has located game birds by their scent. And, then, all that breeding and all that training having paid off in a perfect point, the hunter can walk in, gun at the ready, and flush the bird. Once it is on the wing, he can shoot it and, if the dog has been so trained, wait while the dead bird is retrieved to him. Without a dog to locate the birds by scent, the hunter would be

113

reduced to blundering through the fields until he startled a bird which would then flush. It would all be very much a hit-and-miss affair, tiring and aimless and mainly a matter of blind luck mixed with perseverance. The bigger the country hunted, the truer all this would be. In the South, in the big grass country where quail are hunted, you simply could not go without a dog.

So, the dog is necessary and functional. But so is any working animal and, past a certain age, no one gets very sentimental about livestock. They have their place, their part to play, and there isn't too much more to be made of it. An animal doing what its instincts tell it to do isn't something most people get choked up about.

But people who own them do get sentimental about bird dogs. Foolishly sentimental. Touchingly sentimental. Thoroughly sentimental.

One of the reasons for this is simple. A good bird dog shares his master's enthusiasm for hunting. The dog works under the discipline of his master's voice and he has been trained, sometimes with a fair amount of force, but he is no barnyard animal who has to be put into harness and goaded into doing an honest day's work. A good bird dog wants to hunt.

Like a lot of hunters who make a pet and a house dog of a bird dog, I have to be careful how I dress during hunting season. I can't put my hunting clothes on first thing in the morning if I plan on doing some work and then going hunting. Once the dog sees those clothes, she goes frantic, barking and turning in circles by the door, waiting for me to go out. If I open the door to the car, she will be inside like a rocket and will not come out just because I ask her to. She acts like she thinks I might have another bird dog stashed somewhere and that I'm spending time in secret with this rival. She does the same thing if she sees a gun, or a gun case, shotgun shell, or even the orange hat I wear in the field.

In the hot, early part of the season, especially in the South, hunters have to watch their dogs carefully to make sure that they don't work themselves too hard. A big pointer that likes to run and run wide, looking for scent, will often go until he drops—sometimes dead from a heart attack or dying of heat stroke. Any pointer will hunt brambles until its tail, which moves until the dog strikes point, is beaten and scratched, dripping with blood. Any good dog will hunt with cut pads or long rips in its skin from barbed wire. Dogs that are trained for it, will go into water that is iced over, whether to retrieve or simply to get across to the other side and hunt some good-looking cover there.

A good bird dog, in short, wants to hunt and find game and many hunters find themselves enthused by the dog, borrowing a little of that absolutely instinctive blood urge on mornings when it is a little too cold or too wet and walking through the briars seems like something less than the best way to spend a day. Hunters honestly feel like they can't let their dogs down. Anyone who hunts has seen it over and over again.

It will get to the point where a man hates to look over at his dog after he has missed an easy shot and, when he can finally bring himself to do it, he will say, "Sorry, girl. I blew it." His tone will be meek. And if there are several of these misses, the man will honestly worry that he is embarrassing his dog and that if it keeps up the dog may refuse to hunt for him anymore. It sounds silly to non-hunters or to people who don't know about hunting with dogs, but it happens all the time.

You will see small but rigid codes of behavior grow up in the dealings a man has with his dog. I know a man who has a dog with a splendid nose, which ordinarily gives a dog confidence to run hard and wide. Instead, his dog is almost too sensitive, and shows an almost visible fear of flushing birds wild. The dog is an excruciatingly careful hunter. Which is fine for the ruffed grouse country where it is hunted.

At any rate, this dog checks everything and if he smells something that just might be a bird, well then he flashes a point. If the scent doesn't check out, he will come off the point and move on. He will often hold one of the false points for a minute or more before deciding that whatever it is he smells, it isn't a grouse or woodcock.

Some hunters would call this a fault. My friend considers it a virtue. "I'd rather have him investigate everything. I'll take the time lost on false points over the time lost trying to figure where the bird that flushed wild went. I'll make that trade every time."

This position leads him to a rule of conduct that he obeys inflexibly when he is in the field. "I honor every point," he says. "I don't want the dog to think I don't have confidence in him."

This man also has a rule about not shooting at birds that flush wild. "His job is to point and my job is to shoot and we have to be a team. There can't be any freelancing. I know how I'd feel if he started hunting for himself."

This man virtually never raises his voice at his dog . . . but he talks to him almost constantly. And the dog, for his part, looks back at his master every few seconds, as if to make sure that he is keeping up and hasn't taken a fall back there somewhere, two legs being so much more unsteady than four.

This kind of attachment is normal enough but it does not come automatically. It comes with time and experience and many days together in the field. Generally it starts when the hunter looks at a litter of pups and picks one.

———•———

You can buy an adult dog, trained and finished. For busy men who want to hunt but don't have time for dog training, this certainly makes sense. But if you can afford the time, a pup pays off in the long run.

Before you buy either a puppy or an adult dog, you have to decide what kind of dog you want. To a large degree, that depends on what sort of birds you will be hunting and in what sort of cover. Also, how you plan to hunt. That is, will you be on horseback or in a jeep, looking for quail in Georgia? Or will you be on foot, looking for woodcock and grouse in tight hilly coverts around New Hampshire? And, if so, how durable are you?

English pointers and English setters are the big running dogs you would pick for the bobwhite in Georgia. Pointers, particularly, are known as wide-ranging, fast-working, hard-charging dogs more interested in finding birds than in making friends. The hound in them shows and they can take a heavy hand when they are being trained or disciplined. The handlers who run the big strings at the quail plantations around Thomasville, Georgia, all carry a leather strap that they use to beat both the bushes and the dogs. They beat the bushes to make birds fly and they beat the dogs when they have broken a point and made the birds fly before the shooters could arrive.

I remember one day hunting in the area around Tallahassee, Florida, as a guest at one of those wonderful shooting plantations. I was up on a mule wagon, with my wife and the driver, watching as the plantation manager and dog handler rode saddle horses and worked a pair of three-year-old pointers through the slash pine and palmettos. Those dogs made wide casts but they always came back and they never ran away. And fast as they went, you could somehow tell that they weren't just running for the pleasure of it, the way some dogs will, but were hunting and doing it seriously.

One of the dogs struck and went into a point that looked like it had been stiffened with wire. One moment the dog had been all motion and now he was stationary as stone. The other dog backed on sight. The handler reined in his horse and raised his hat, a signal to the wagon driver that the dogs were on point.

"Look at that," I said to my wife. "You ever see anything so pretty?"

She agreed that it was impressive.

"Like somebody painted it," I said. We'd been getting work like that out of these two dogs for the last hour. This was their fourth covey.

I had my eyes on the dogs as I started to climb down from the wagon. While I watched, the dog that had struck the birds broke point and ran in, scattering the covey.

"Whoa," the handler yelled.

The dog ran a little farther and then stopped.

The handler dismounted, walked over to the dog, grabbed a handful of flesh from around its neck, and lifted the dog in the air. Then he went to work with the leather strap.

"Whoa, Bell," he would say, then whip the dog across its flank with the leather strap. *Crack.*

"Whoa, Bell." *Crack.*

"Whoa, Bell." *Crack.*

The dog took maybe a dozen licks with the strap. It was such an ordinary piece of business that the dog never whimpered and the handler never spat out his cheekful of tobacco. And when the whipping was done, the dog went back onto a long cast into the palmettos and the handler remounted his horse and that was that.

"Tough dogs," my wife said.

"The toughest," I said, repeating the conventional wisdom. Everyone always said that pointers were hardheaded and tough as nails and we'd just had a very convincing demonstration. I told her about the man I'd once seen shoot his pointer with a load of nines for chasing a rabbit. The shot didn't penetrate but it had to sting. The dog never whimpered. It stopped chasing the rabbit but I couldn't be sure that wasn't because it was afraid the next shot might come from closer range, with sixes. Some hunters, sadly, do discipline dogs by shooting them. They fail to understand the distinction between discipline and revenge.

———— • ————

The conventional wisdom about pointers, it turns out, is more conventional than wise. I learned this talking to a man who has trained bird dogs all over the country and whose name is known in both field trial and hunting circles as one of the very best. He is retired now and when I take my dog over to him, he has some time for talk.

One day I told him about the pointer I'd seen whipped and said something about what hardheaded, wide-ranging dogs they were. I'd said it to be saying something the trainer would automatically have to agree with, to make us more nearly equals. Like meeting a professional baseball player and remarking that Nolan Ryan throws with a lot of speed.

The trainer, to my surprise, said, "You know that's not always true about pointers. One of the best, close-working grouse dogs I've ever had was a pointer."

"Come on," I said, not knowing when to quit. "Must have been an old dog."

"Not at all. And I got the dog from a man who said he couldn't do anything with it. That every time he put the dog out all he was interested in doing was watching the ground go rolling under his belly."

"You must have had to come down mighty hard on that dog to get him to hunt grouse." The conventional wisdom knows no limits.

"Actually," the trainer said, "I made a house dog out of him."

I decided to shut up and listen.

Most pointers, the trainer agreed, are wide and headstrong dogs. It is in the breeding of most of them, and in the training of all the ones you see hunting quail on the big plantations. "When you've got ten thousand acres or more to hunt," he said, "you want dogs that can cover ground.

"And as for being hardheaded," he went on, "how many dogs did they have on that plantation you hunted?"

"Twenty-eight."

"And one handler to train them and work them, right? The only way you can do that is to come down hard on a dog. It's one of the reasons people like pointers. You can use a firm hand and the dog won't fall apart on you. But that's not the only way."

He'd made the running pointer he was given into a house dog. Let him sleep next to the bed. Took him everywhere he went. After a few months of this treatment, the dog was afraid to let him out of sight. Then he worked him for a while with a check cord, keeping the dog in close. And finally, when it came time to hunt grouse, he had a close-working pointer.

"Of course that's not for everyone. You have to spend a lot of time with a dog and you have to know a lot about dogs. But it can be done. I always liked that saying 'You can take it out of them, but you can't put it in them.' You can work with a big running, headstrong dog and get him to work to the guns a lot sooner than you can take a lazy dog that wants to stay underfoot and make him go out and hunt birds."

This is *not* to say that the English pointer should be your choice if you are looking for a dog for hunting grouse. Only that the stereotypes are as unilluminating when it comes to dogs as they are with just about everything else.

———————•———————

The main breeds of pointing dogs are the English pointer, English setter, German shorthair, and Brittany spaniel. There are some other breeds around. Gordon setters. Vizslas. Weimaraners. Every breed has certain characteristics. And within every breed, there are typical and atypical lines. Good dogs and worthless dogs. There are general rules and exceptions to every one of them.

Field trial results would tend to bear out that the pointer is probably the finest pure performer. But many hunters prefer setters for their looks—less visible hound in their background and the long feathery coat is appealing to look at. Also, setters are thought to be a little more affectionate and demonstrative than the all-business pointer. On the other hand, there are those who say that setters can be more high-strung and unpredictable—more likely to run away just when you least want them to—and that the coat might look good but it sure does pick up a lot of burrs. Both dogs, it is generally agreed, can be strong, determined, hardworking bird finders in the field. You just have to get the right dog and make sure he's well trained and worked a lot. Which makes it sound easy.

The German dogs are said to be a little less vigorous, a little closer working, and a little less single-minded about finding birds. This is because they were bred to hunt virtually anything that could be hunted on the country estates. Rabbits and stags included. Also,

the breeders worked on their retrieving capabilities as well since they were expected to pick up ducks. So the shorthair and weimaraner are said to be good medium-range dogs, excellent for the Midwest where they can hunt pheasant, quail, and grouse. They are also considered good pets—which is not thought to be true of pointers, particularly, and setters a little less so.

The Brittany spaniel is the smallest of the pointing dogs and, so, tends to hunt close without having to be broken or trained especially to do it. (But there is one Brittany owner—me—who will assure you that when one of these dogs wants to run off, there is no holding it back.) The Brittany is, therefore, considered especially good for grouse and woodcock in tight covers. However, some hunters use Brittanys on quail, especially if they are hunting smaller fields. These dogs make excellent pets. They might be the best choice if you want a dog that can double as a house dog and a hunting dog.

Those are generalities, of course. Before you decide on a dog, it would be wise first to research the breed and then the line to make sure of what you are getting. In the end, it will help to have as much science as possible influencing your decision since you will tend to go with preferences you either can't explain or wouldn't care to. Some hunters just can't bring themselves to hunt with a Brittany because the dog is too damned small. It's like hunting with a toy. Others will take the setter over the pointer because the pointer looks a little too much like the hounds they see chained up in farmer's yards. And still others will want a German shorthair because it is the dog they remember from a thousand calendars.

When it comes to the actual dog—not the generalities of the breed—you need to research the line. If you can go back a few generations and find a field trial champion, then you are lucky and while your worries are not over, you can feel better about taking a dog out of that line. You can talk to people who've bought littermates. You can look into the reputation of the breeder. And if you are buying a finished adult dog, you can ask for a demonstration.

A lot of oldtimers used to say that the runt of any litter usually made the best hunter. I never heard it explained why this should be so. I, for one, am inclined to believe there might be something to it just because I've heard it so often. Other than that dubious piece of advice, and the obvious cautions of not taking a pup that doesn't seem active or energetic, you are more or less on your own once you've decided to take a pup from the litter of what you are sure are well-bred pups.

It has been established fairly conclusively, however, that you ought to take the pup shortly after it has been weaned. By the seventh week. According to extensive research, pups that are socialized early are much more tractable than those that leave the litter late. And those that stay with the bitch past four months can become virtually untrainable. The earlier they start, the easier it is for dogs to become accustomed to the mysterious business of dealing with humans.

This method makes good sense for the man who intends to work one dog that will live in and around the house and be as much companion as working dog. He can train the dog and then send him out. On the other hand, there is the professional with a kennel full of dogs to train and work who prefers to let the young dog run hard and build up his enthusiasm and then break him to his command at two years. This is the classic method and it works well. Trainer brings the dog in instead of sending him out.

The writers who encourage you to begin training your pup at seven or eight weeks inevitably stress the benefits of the early start and they always have the dog in mind. There is general agreement that early training gets the pup used to obedience at an age and size when defiance is unthinkable. And that the pup therefore learns early that things go better when he tries to please.

All this makes good logical sense. It is also backed up by the studies and by the first-hand experience of many dog owners, including this one. But I think it overlooks something.

It is also good for the human to start early. You do not feel the same way about a puppy that you do about a full-grown dog. The size of the puppy and its vulnerability bring something out in the handler. You want the pup to do well and you are encouraging. You coax and compliment and overlook mistakes. You find training sessions fun and the pup's enthusiasm infectious. And this side of you is probably imprinted on his young, quickly forming brain. He comes to think of you as an okay sort of fellow, someone it is possible to get along with. Consider this argument by analogy: which is more fun, teaching your baby son how to walk or your teenaged son (same kid) how to drive? And doesn't it make it easier to teach the teenager how to drive if you once taught him to walk?

Working with a puppy should be fun for both of you. The experts stress that fifteen minutes a day is about right until the dog is nearly full grown. Any more than that taxes the dog's attention span and takes the fun out of it. You can sour the dog on the whole business of hunting if you go too long and push too hard.

In the fifteen-minute sessions, you should teach your dog the basic obedience commands and then work with him on pointing and retrieving, using a bird wing on a fishing rod and a retrieving dummy. A puppy of nine or ten weeks can be taught to point the bird wing once he has learned the command "Whoa." This is a long way from pointing live birds in the wild but it is a great start and it does make for a tight bond between dog and master.

If you are going to train a dog, you should educate yourself concerning training methods. It is beyond the scope of a general book such as this to go into all the techniques and the theory. There are different schools and there are subtle points that you should consider before you start training a pup. It wouldn't be a bad idea to get to know someone who has had some success working with dogs and ask every fool question that comes into your head before you start trying to train a dog yourself. When something comes up, you will know where to go for advice. It is important that you do not proceed blindly in training a dog, doing things because they seem to make sense. It is possible to ruin a dog or at least develop bad habits that cannot be broken except—if at all—through considerable retraining.

I found this out when I talked to the retired trainer who keeps and works my dog from time to time. I told him how I had been working with my dog to make sure that she didn't become gun shy—taking her out and shooting a small-bore shotgun when she was with me to get her used to the sound—and he said, "You're lucky you didn't *make* her gun shy doing that."

I asked him how that could happen. Wasn't it the idea to get the dog used to the gun?

Not exactly, he said. The idea was to get the dog to the point where it didn't *notice* the sound of the gun or, if it did, it associated that sound with something it liked. If you started just shooting guns, surprising the dog with the sound for no reason at all, like you were sneaking up to it and saying *boo*, then pretty soon the dog would get nervous every time it saw the gun come out, knowing that sooner or later you were going to shoot the thing, just when it was least expected.

"It's amazing the number of dogs I get," the trainer went on, "that are here because somebody did something wrong and now he wants me to fix it." He showed me a fine-looking lemon-and-white pointer in one of his kennels and said, "Take that dog there. He's one of the worst blinkers I've ever seen."

"Blinker?"

"That's a dog that when he smells birds, he blinks and walks around them. He knows the birds are there but he won't point them *or* flush them."

"Come on," I said. "Dogs want to rush birds. It takes some discipline to point them but it would take *more* to blink them."

"That's right. But if you make it unpleasant enough for a dog, every time he shows you he's smelled birds, then he'll stop showing you he's smelled them. The way it happens is the dog makes a mistake and crowds a covey of birds—or just one bird—and the owner comes down on him like a ton of bricks. He gets nervous and does it again and he gets another load dropped on him. Pretty soon he stops crowding birds and walks all the way around them. You see it a lot with shock collars. People who don't know how to use them will hit a dog with them when they make a mistake on pointing. Pretty soon the dog learns not to point. I use collars but I don't use them to steady a dog. I'll use them on a dog that's running away and won't turn when I call him. You only have to do it once or twice.

"The fellow who owns that lemon-and-white dog brought him to me and said he couldn't do anything with the dog. He didn't think the dog had a nose. So I put some quail out in the field and turned the dog loose. He was perfect on those birds, smelled all of them and walked around every one of them wide enough so none of them flushed. He couldn't have done it if he'd had a bad nose. I called the fellow up and asked him if he'd used a shock collar on the dog and he said, 'Well, yes, but only when he made a bad mistake, like breaking in on birds.' So I told him he'd made a blinker out of a dog that had a lot of potential."

Could he make the dog right? I asked.

"Oh, maybe. But it's a lot harder than just training him to point. Like you say, blinking takes more skill than pointing. And the dog will never be as good as he could have been."

The lesson is that you can ruin a dog if you don't know what you are doing or even if you do but aren't sure of the limits to a method or the tolerance of your dog. A professional knows how much force any one dog can take and how much is needed. And, because he knows dogs and what to expect from them, he never loses his temper. On my little Brittany, the trainer never uses much more than a stern word and a hard look. On some big pointers, he gets out the shock collar and the strap. So you should read up and get in touch with somebody who knows what he is doing before you start training a dog yourself.

All the preceding is, also, one more argument for starting with your dog as a pup if you can afford the time. On the one hand you will learn something about the dog's temperament and know just how much discipline the dog can take and how firm you should be. Also, the discipline will of necessity be mild at first. Not many people can come down hard on a little puppy and the whole dynamic between master and dog will be one where the dog tries to please and the master rewards good behavior. It is a good way, I think, to cut down on the number of blinkers in the world.

A final word. Every hunter expects too much of his first dog, no matter how well that dog performs. No dog is perfect and even the best dogs make mistakes. And not just mistakes of technique, either. Fundamental, bonehead mistakes. Like the pointer who rushed a covey on the plantation near Tallahassee that day. Much of what a dog does is natural but the actual point is not. What the dog *wants* to do is creep in on the game he has located. What he has been trained against his instincts to do is point that game and wait for you to come along and do the killing. Sometimes the dog just can't control his instincts any longer. Dogs will break in on pointed birds and they will chase rabbits and they will do all sorts of things that the wild, instinctive side of them wants to do. You can almost see it in the face of a dog who decides to go ahead and break the rules. There is an expression that says, "Ah, what the hell. I'll get a beating for it but just this once, it's worth it."

The more you hunt with dogs the higher your tolerance will be for these lapses and, in some rule of consequence, the fewer of them there will be. Too much pressure on a dog is like too much pressure on a human—it causes mistakes in the clutch. Old-time hunters love their dogs as much for their faults as for their virtues (within limits) and this allows everyone to relax and have a good time. It can diminish a hunt considerably if a dog owner is constantly yelling at his dog and correcting it and trying to make it behave according to some abstract notion of perfection.

After you have hunted with a dog, or many dogs, for a while you lose some of the urge for perfection and can take what the dog does, mistakes included, as part of the fine package that bird hunting is.

You will also feel something for another creature that you probably never would have thought possible.

12

Dressed and Ready

Bird hunters use up much of their passion for gear and tools when they decide on a gun—or guns—and a dog. Compared to trout fishermen, say, the average bird hunter is an ascetic when it comes to clothing and equipment. To look at the average bird hunter, in fact, you would think he gives absolutely no thought to what he wears and carries into the field with him. But this would be going too far.

You do need to dress for the work. The gunners at the fashionable Edwardian shoots *dressed*. Plus fours, leggings, neckties, and tweed jackets. The only permissible eccentricity was in the matter of head gear. One shooter said of another, "By jove! I am not a wealthy man, but I would willingly give 1,000 pounds to have the impertinent audacity to wear that hat."

Of course, that was another day and, more importantly, a different style of hunting. You have to doubt that even the stuffiest Englishman would be willing to dive into the briars and muck of a good American grouse cover, wearing tweeds and a four-in-hand.

The rule for the American upland bird hunter is comfort and protection. Which means that before he decides on what to wear, the hunter has to know where and when he will be hunting.

The early days of the bird season can be as warm as the warmest day in summer. You will want to wear the lightest clothing you can get by with. But the briars and the brush will be at their most evil during these days—they feed on sunlight, after all—so you will want protection. Something to turn the briars. Poplin pants faced with canvas and a canvas shirt, heavy canvas vest, should do it. Even so, you will be hot and sweaty and the high briars will cut at your neck and hands. The especially stubborn briars will tear your shirt.

As the season wears on and the days turn a little colder, you can switch to the heavier duck canvas. You can also wear pants that are faced with heavier material—cordura, for instance, will turn briars and is indestructible, but it does not breathe. Gloves are a great help to the grouse hunter because he will be fighting brush and briars and, when his hands are protected, he will be inclined to go where otherwise he might not. And the birds are often in the toughest cover. A full hunting jacket may help, though it takes a genuinely cold day to call for one of those. The walking you do for birds will keep you warm even when there is ice on the potholes.

The walking you must do is what calls for the most careful choice of clothing. The worst briar cuts are as nothing compared to blisters on your feet. You'll want to be sure about your boots.

Traditionally, bird hunters owned a pair for dry hunting and another for those days when they expected to get wet. The dry boots were all leather, moccasin-styled lace-ups that came about ten inches up the calf. Very lightweight and very well made, they felt good on your feet, if they were properly fitted, and if you saddle-soaped them now and then to clean the leather, and kept it well lubricated with mink oil or bear grease, then the boots would last forever and take on some real character. They became almost a second pair of feet.

The footwear of choice for wet work was some variation on the boot made popular by L. L. Bean—rubber bottoms stitched to leather uppers. This has been one of the most popular pieces of footwear in history and it does well at what it is designed to do. It is light and dry and well made.

Recently, new developments in the synthetic-fabrics industry have made it possible for one boot to do the work of both. A leather boot can be lined with a sock made of Gore Tex or one of the other breathable but waterproof synthetics to give the hunter a boot that

is comfortable and waterproof and does not get as wet on the inside, from the body's own moisture, as those with rubber bottoms often do.

There were some problems with the early lined leather boots and a lot of hunters became skeptics. But the bugs have been worked out of the system. I was asked last year to "field test" a pair of these lined boots and was entirely and pleasantly satisfied.

Make sure your boots fit with whatever kind of sock you will customarily wear in the field. Keep them oiled, if only to prevent stiffening of the leather, which can be as uncomfortable for your feet as it is bad for the leather.

If you settle on a good pair of properly fitting boots lined with one of the synthetics, that should take care of your needs for footwear unless you hunt in snake country and cannot go into the field without seeing visions of a five-foot diamondback nailing you in the calf just as the covey flushes. A good pair of snake boots will buy you a lot of peace of mind. For many hunters, this is worth the price even if they wear them for thirty years and never even see a snake.

Another piece of safety apparel worth considering is a pair of good glasses. In the old days, shooters wore some kind of protection for their eyes because the powders were not always reliable and there was a chance a chunk of it, half burned, would blow back into your face. That is not a danger these days but if you hunt upland birds, especially grouse or woodcock, then there are still hazards you should protect yourself against.

A few seasons back, when my dog was young and needed to be worked every day (the sacrifices we bird hunters make) I was easing up into a cleared section of one of my favorite coverts, looking for the dog. Her bell had stopped and I was sure she was on point close by somewhere. I had both hands on the gun and was using it, as well as my feet and the top of my head, to push the head-high bull briars out of my way. There was a sudden sound to my left and I turned, mounting the gun to shoot the grouse I was sure was getting up. But it was just a woodpecker. I turned back in the direction I had been going, took one step, and got slapped full in the face by a briar shoot that I'd been holding down with my foot and had forgotten about in all the excitement. It hurt enough that I almost dropped the gun.

Instead, I sat down and dabbed at my tearing eye for ten minutes with a bandanna. It cleared up enough that I hunted out the covert and one or two more. But that night at dinner, the eye began to tear again and this time it would not stop. It ran all night and the next morning the doctor had to pull the tiny tip of a thorn out of my cornea, which was badly scratched. The eye had to be bandaged for several days while the cornea healed. It did, completely—so I suppose I am lucky; but I sure did hate to deprive my dog of all those hunting days. Needless to say, none of it would have happened if I had been wearing shooting glasses. Orvis sells glasses with shot-proof lenses and one day a local hunter came into the company's retail store in Manchester saying he wanted to buy a dozen pair. Turned out he had been wearing the glasses himself the previous weekend when a hunting partner caught him in the face with most of his shot pattern. He was badly stung and frightened, but without the glasses he would have been blinded. There is no record of what he did to that particular partner but he said everyone he ever hunted with in the future would be wearing a pair of those shot-proof glasses.

Some hunters say they would wear glasses if they could keep them from fogging but they can't, since they walk hard and sweat a lot and the glasses inevitably get steamed over. You can buy either a stick from the sporting goods store or a solution from the auto supply store to prevent this. No shooter should be indifferent to the protection of his eyes. He can, does, and even should abuse other parts of his body, but his eyes are sacred.

A hat isn't so crucial but it is a piece of gear that hunters seem to take seriously, perhaps as a holdover from the tradition of the big driven shoots. A hunter's hat says something about his personality. Some hats, obviously, cannot be worn in tight cover. The baseball style hat with its high crown and long bill is always catching limbs and leaving the hunter's head. So you want something that does not keep your mind constantly on your hat. But other than that, the world of headgear is open to you and your talent and taste for eccentricity. It isn't a bad idea to make your hat a piece of safety gear. Wear one made of blaze orange so that your partners—and anyone else who happens to be in the woods—will know where you are and that you are not fair game. Keep the bill of your cap to less than three inches; otherwise you will have to raise your head to see a fuller picture.

In the pockets of his pants and vest, the bird hunter will carry a few indispensable tools. A knife, of course. You'll want to carry a knife in the woods, always. A bird hunter might want to carry one of those that comes with a straight blade and a gut hook so he can draw his birds in the field if he is hunting on a very hot day.

He will also want to carry a compass. It is entirely possible to get yourself lost while hunting birds even if you know you are within a mile of your car because you were hunting from the time you parked it. You might also want to carry a topo map, especially if you do not know the country or have come to it looking for new bird cover. A good reading of the contour lines can sometimes tell you where to look.

In the South, some hunters carry a snake-bite kit, though the new thinking on the subject is that the best snake-bite kit of all is a set of car keys. If you get hit by a rattler, don't waste time fooling around with tourniquets and suction and cutting little X's over the fang marks. Just get yourself to the nearest emergency room and turn the problem over to experts.

Some hunters carry food or water. The water, especially, isn't a bad idea since you'll get thirsty if you are out long and more and more, the temptation to drink from the inviting wild streams should be resisted. A new kind of parasite called Giardilla has been on the move. It first showed up in the West but has been identified more or less everywhere now. Beavers seem to be the host organism so if you drink downstream from a beaver dam, unawares, you could come down with something that is as debilitating and serious as amoebic dysentery.

Out West, hunters will carry binoculars so they can glass the big fields and the arroyos before they hunt them. Given the amount of country there is to hunt, this is the only way to decide whether a field is worth the effort or not.

Chapstick. Whistle for the dog. Bandanna to wipe your sweaty brow. Tobacco if you use it. Except for some shells there shouldn't be much more that you will need in the field.

You'll want to keep some water in the car for your dog. This can be very important in the early part of the season when the dogs are running hard and having a tough time throwing off all the heat. Hunters get hot, too, and a cooler with some tea or lemonade is welcome after three or four hours in the field. And, at the end of the day, when there is no more gunning to be done, the cold beers in the cooler will taste awfully good.

The properly outfitted and equipped bird hunter may not be much to look at (this seems to be the effect he desires, in fact) but there is a point to most of what he wears and carries—with the possible exception of the hat. If he will never become a fashion figure, the way the cowboy and the Maine fishing guide have, then all the better. Nobody wants people coming into the field just so they can wear the clothes. As long as the birds and your dog do not object to what you look like, then wear what works and feels good. Outside of bird hunting, you won't get many chances.

13

The Game Cook

You eat what you shoot. Or you should, anyway. And at the very least, if you absolutely can't stand game, you ought to give what you shoot to another hunter who appreciates it. The sheer fact that you have gone to the trouble to go into the field and hunt down the birds that you've killed requires that you treat them with respect once they are on the ground. This means making them into meals that are worthy of them and of your efforts. Virtually every bird hunter I've ever known has enjoyed eating game and couldn't imagine the sport without the meal that consummates the hunt.

Leigh Perkins has made a near lifetime study of game cookery and, having tasted birds that he has cooked, I am willing to bow to his experience and proven skill. What follows are his recommendations regarding handling, hanging, cleaning, and cooking game birds.

Birds that have been badly damaged should probably be cleaned immediately to avoid spoilage. Smaller birds—quail and woodcock—need not be drawn before they are hung provided they are in good shape. Larger birds—grouse, pheasant, and turkey—do better, on the other hand, if they are drawn before being hung.

The hanging of a bird is done to allow enzymes to break down fibers and tenderize the meat. It is commonly done with beef and it works on game, too. The birds should be hung in relatively cool temperatures—35 to 55 degrees—and be protected against flies. If this is not possible outside, then some kind of cooler or refrigerating system is advised. The bird should be hung from the head—or from the feet if it has been drawn. It should never be hung from the feet if it has not been drawn.

The length of time the bird is allowed to hang is a matter of some dispute. The French, who know about cooking, will leave a pheasant hanging by the neck, undrawn, for a week, until the flesh is so high it actually comes apart and the bird falls. When plucked, portions of the bird's carcass will have turned green. This is a little much for most Americans.

Perkins believes that birds should be left hanging for at least four days and possibly as long as six. For turkey the range is five to seven days.

When it is time to take the birds down you should carefully pluck them by pulling the feathers with the grain and then singeing

any small pin feathers with a low gas flame. Then open the cavity with a sharp-pointed knife and clean the viscera out with your fingers. Wipe the cavity and wash to remove the clotted blood. This reduces the chance of bacterial invasions.

Serious hunters will from time to time have more game than they can reasonably hang or eat. They need to store it somehow. Freezing is the way everyone goes these days, though there is some argument about what is the best way to freeze birds. Most people who are serious about the thing say that the worst way is to put plucked birds in a plastic bag and freeze them. That way there's too much risk of freezer burn, of the fat turning rancid, and of the flesh deteriorating over time.

The most commonly used alternative is to pluck the birds and freeze them in water. The ice protects them against burn and against drying out and does a good job of keeping the meat in condition to eat. A less popular alternative but one with some fierce advocates is freezing the birds unplucked. You draw them (a very few hunters omit this step) and take off the heads and feet, then put the birds in bags and freeze them with the feathers still on. According to the people who use this system, it does the best job of preserving the meat and also prevents freezer burn. No matter what method is used, game birds should not be frozen for longer than six to eight months—four months with very fatty birds such as woodcock. After this much time, the fat will turn.

Whatever method you use, birds that have been stored improperly can be saved. One of the best ways is to bone them and grind them up in a processor and then add such ingredients as you think will make a good pâté. You can also use damaged birds, along with the bones of birds already eaten, to make a fine game-bird stock. Small parts that come off in the cleaning—the legs of woodcock, say—can be collected over a season and, when you have enough, deep fried as one-bite hors d'oeuvres. Livers and hearts and gizzards make fine hors d'oeuvres and some aficionados go so far as to eat the sautéed intestines of woodcock—which they call, euphemistically, "trail." You do not, however, have to go this far to enjoy the taste of game.

———————•———————

When it comes to cooking, there are many cookbooks that contain recipes for wild game. Many of them are just awful. Reject out of hand any book that tells you how to prepare the game so as to tenderize it. You will see some of these books go so far as to recommend boiling a bird before roasting it. This is an abomination.

For years, the uninformed but prevalent thinking about game was that it had to be cooked well done to make it palatable. In other words, the natural flavors of game were to be suppressed by excessive cooking. Or by a long session in a marinade before cooking. And you still run across people who believe this.

But game has wonderful flavors that nothing else can match and if you don't want to taste those flavors you should avoid eating game rather than cook it until those flavors are destroyed.

As a rule of thumb, small birds should be cooked hot and quick and the larger birds should be cooked cool and slow. It is important to remember that wild birds are lean and muscled, unlike domestically raised birds. You can easily cook the moisture right out of game birds and be left with something dry, tough, and unappetizing. The best way to avoid this is to keep the inside of the meat cool (within limits) and the best way to do that is to use a device called Thermicator and a companion book called *Game Cookery: Based on Internal Temperature* by Leigh Perkins. Both are available, not surprisingly, through Orvis. The Thermicator is a kind of meat thermometer that does not require the large shaft of the older-styled models, so you can check the temperature of your birds without damaging them. The book tells you the best internal temperatures for the various types of game birds and how to prepare them. I have field-tested the recipes as executed by the author and they produce just what they claim to: very tasty birds.

You can do it neat, as Perkins does. For instance, he charcoals quail and the recipe is as follows:

Split quail up back or up breast. Either works. If split up the breast, the meat lies flatter. If split up the back, the breast is intact. Dip bird in melted butter or baste with butter. Salt and pepper and place on grill for about three or four minutes on each side. Here is where the Thermicator is a must because one minute means the difference between success or failure. Internal temperature: 140 to 150.

I have eaten quail prepared just that way, in the field, and they are wonderful. They were also good that way when I ate them at the dining-room table.

At another extreme, you can make up woodcock and oysters, as my wife does them:

Skin twelve woodcock breasts, then fillet each side from the breast bone. Lightly dust with flour seasoned with salt and pepper, and put aside while you sauté two large shallots in two tablespoons of butter. When shallots are tender, but not brown, remove them from the pan with a slotted spoon and reserve. Add a bit more butter, turn up the heat, and sauté the woodcock breasts quick and hot (no more than a minute or two on each side). Remove and reserve with the shallots in a heated container.

Deglaze pan with one-quarter cup of good quality Madeira to make a light sauce. Add one pint oysters and cook only until the edges curl.

Now combine the shallots, woodcock breasts, oysters, and Madeira sauce. Taste and quickly correct seasoning. (You may need more salt and pepper or you may want to add a touch of ground thyme.)

Serve on toast points as a first course or with wild rice as an entrée.

The dish must be made quickly and served immediately. It cannot be allowed to stand.

This dish is also excellent but not to be served (wasted on) anyone who is neither a bold eater nor a lover of game, which may amount to the same thing.

If you have several game birds and want to blend them into something novel, you might want to try this little game-bird pâté.

You begin by cutting strips of breast meat about a quarter of an inch wide and marinating them in cognac with some allspice, thyme, salt, pepper, and chopped shallots added.

Meanwhile, grind two cups of the meat of whatever bird you are using and two cups of fatty pork in a food processor. (Sometimes known as the Cuisinart.) Season with sautéed shallots and garlic. Also salt, pepper, allspice, and thyme. Add two eggs for consistency. Then add the marinade, in which the quarter-inch strips have been soaking.

Now, line your baking dish, or dishes, with bacon or thinly sliced pork fat and begin layering in the meat mixture and the marinated quarter-inch strips. Top and bottom should be the meat mixture with the strips alternating in between. Cover with more bacon or pork fat and a layer of foil. Weight the dish and place in a pan of boiling water in a 350-degree oven for an hour and a half or until the juices run clear. Cool while still weighted.

The red meat/red wine, white meat/white wine rule applies to game birds. Dove and woodcock and sharptail call for a Cabernet Sauvignon or a Bordeaux. Quail or ruffed grouse go best with Chardonnay.

What you serve with game is important and you will probably find the rich harvest-season vegetables and side dishes make good complements to your birds. Winter squash, asparagus, chestnuts, wild rice, sweet potatoes.

Game birds, because they are something out of the ordinary,

make a good main course for a dinner party. But be sure that your guests actually *like* game before you invite them over for grouse and white grapes in a wine sauce. There are people who, unlikely as it may seem, simply do not like game. And there are people who like some game but not all game.

If you invite the right people, however, people who enjoy eating game and also enjoy the idea of the hunt, then you can have some wonderful times around the table, eating birds you have shot. There is something a little primitive about it. Something to remind you that it wasn't always as easy as simply going to the supermarket.

Cooking and eating game puts you in mind of a feast and a celebration, and when you bring home game that you have killed, you will know, better than you ever have, the pride of the provider.

14

Getting
Started

Perhaps a summing up is in order. With many alternatives on the table, how is the newcomer to chose among them? How does he get started? What does he buy and where? What does he need to learn and where can be go to learn it?

If a friend of mine decided that he wanted to take up bird hunting and asked me for some advice, here's what I would tell him:

First I would satisfy myself that he really wanted to hunt and not just shoot. An awful lot of people can be satisfied with breaking clay birds on a skeet or trap range and do not need to go into the woods to hunt real game. As short as the supply of wild game and huntable land is, there isn't any reason for someone to be out there who doesn't really want to be. Bird hunting is not golf.

So, once the new hunter has acquired the minimal shooting skills and demonstrated a proper reverence for gun safety—perhaps by going to one of the shooting schools—I would probably send him to a preserve and let him try his hand on real, flesh-and-blood birds. I would make the hunt as realistic as possible and I would try to get the preserve to use one of its best dogs. If, after the day in the preserve's planted fields, shooting its planted birds, my friend still wanted more, then we would talk about hunting some wild birds.

At this point, it would probably be smart to start talking shotguns and equipment. Nobody does anything these days without wanting to acquire the gear. The passion for the equipment comes immediately to life.

So, we would talk about guns. I would not presume to tell someone exactly what gun to buy but I would tell him that he can do all the upland bird shooting he wants to do with a good twenty-gauge double (he may want a twelve for pheasant and turkey) and that there is no such thing as a bargain when it comes to guns. A cheap one isn't worth the money and a good one will last for generations and increase in value each year. One good gun, well suited to the hunter and perhaps made to fit, can give him a lifetime of shooting. Going the other way may have him changing guns season after season and finding that each change throws his shooting off that fraction that makes a big difference. Buy carefully, I would say, and try to make your gun something you feel comfortable with in every regard.

For the accessories, the clothing and the boots and the glasses and such, I would probably advise any friend of mine to go to the catalogues and, since this is an Orvis book and since I live just down the road from the Orvis store and generally stop in about three days before bird season starts every year to pick up a new pair of briar-proofs—for the simple reason that I've always been satisfied—I would probably tell my friend that he couldn't go wrong with Orvis stuff.

I know that it is all elaborately field tested by Perkins himself and not a collection of Harvard MBAs who do not shoot and do not care to learn and are merely trying to find the material that turns the most briars for the money. Perkins will be wearing the trousers in some of our local grouse coverts where the briars are enough to break the heart of even the stoutest shooter and dog. He will be more interested in turning every briar than in turning the cost-efficient number of them.

So, I can honestly recommend Orvis gear for bird shooting.

———————•———————

I would tell my friend that a bird covert is not a singles bar and that what he wears should fit loosely—hang not cling—because he will be stretching and reaching and contorting himself into odd shapes to slide under barbed-wire fences and over big blown-down oak trees and that he does not want his clothes to bind. I would also tell him that bird hunting in the early season can be warm work and that he should keep that in mind and buy lightweight stuff where possible, as long as it is also strong. I would tell him, above all, to make sure that his boots fit and that if they are not waterproof to put mink oil on inside and out and not to worry that it stains his socks. I would tell him that, when he buys a vest or jacket, to look for one that has a relatively small number of pockets and shell loops and other such things that can reach out and grab branches and briars at the most inopportune moments. A vest with a game pouch that rides on the small of the back and has zippered pockets will save a lot of discomfort in the woods.

The vest, like everything else he buys, should be good quality. The discount store stuff tends to need replacing every year while the good stuff goes on and on.

I probably would discourage the brand-new bird hunter from buying a dog right away. Spend a season, I would say, going out with other people who have dogs—people who have been doing it for a while and know what they can expect from a dog. People who are genuinely in love with the sport of bird hunting with dogs.

Those people, it seems to me, share one thing above all else and that is a sense that like man, the dog is fallible and, therefore, a fellow creature worthy of love and respect. Something to be admired at times, pitied at times, and laughed at now and then. In short, they do not expect too much and they are grateful when a dog lives up to its potential.

Too many new hunters who are going out with their first dog expect miracles or perfection, which amounts to the same thing. Their ideas of how dogs should perform in the field come from calendar art and breathless stories in the lesser sporting journals and a collection of half truths of dubious ancestry.

Worst of all, these novices think that the performance of the dog is a reflection in some way of their worth. Good man has a good dog.

Dog that won't mind, runs away, and now and then busts in on a covey is a sure sign that his owner is a slovenly soul who cannot be trusted to pay his bills or taxes.

One of the first times I ever went out with a dog I was expecting miracles. Staunch points and stately retrieves, beautiful casts back and forth across the broomweed. A day of near artistic perfection in which I would be both player and spectator. I was fourteen and didn't know anything.

Our dog, a big, hardheaded pointer named Stoney (after Stonewall Jackson), pointed before he was even limber and we shot a couple of birds on the covey rise. It was just as I had expected and I could not have been more satisfied. My companion, the dog's owner, however, was uneasy.

"I don' like it," he said after Stoney had retrieved our birds.

"What's the matter?" I said, trying to sound wise. "Did Stoney hardmouth the birds?"

"Oh, no. Those were good retrieves. It's just that usually he runs about three miles in a great big circle when I let him out of the car. I yell and he ignores me. Then, a little while later, he'll bust the first covey he finds and I'll yell some more. Then he'll false point. Or point a stinkbird or a gopher. And finally, somewhere around midmorning, he'll settle down and start hunting and the rest of the day will go fine. He's a young dog and he'll settle down in another two or three seasons. But this thing today, finding birds right away, it's backwards. It's probably downhill from here on out."

I, of course, didn't believe it. Not until the dog busted a couple of coveys, chased a mule and, finally, rolled around in the very ripe carcass of a dead pig for a full five minutes before we could get up to him. From then on, it was a blessing when the dog ranged far ahead of us and downwind.

If he'd been my dog, I would have fried in my own fury. But my host had owned a lot of dogs in his time and he was partial to big stud pointers and he just smiled the way a tolerant father will smile when he comes home and finds his young hellion of a son has blown up all the garbage cans with illegal fireworks and has been suspended from school for fighting with three older boys. You've got to give them a little head or they'll never know how hard they can run.

So I would tell my beginning friend to wait a year or two before he buys his first dog. He doesn't want to go into the thing with unreasonable expectations and then be frustrated and turned off the sport for good. Also, after a couple of years of hunting, he will have a better idea of what kind of dog he wants and he will start hearing about litters that are coming up. He may have hunted with a dog that he likes and that dog may be coming due. That always helps, to know the blood not just from the papers the owner shows you but from seeing what it translates into in field work.

By the time you have hunted a season or two behind dogs that are not yours and know what to expect from a dog, you will probably be eager to work with a puppy. You can buy some of the good books on the subject while you are waiting for the pups to be weaned and you can drop in and look at the pups at play now and then. It is surprising how much you can tell about the personality and disposition of puppies when they are only a few weeks old. After a few visits you will probably know which one you want.

If you want to start the dog yourself, which is what I would recommend to my friend, you can still send him out for some finish work before his second year, which will be his first real season in the woods. I would also recommend this course. A professional, working serious sessions with a dog, every day, can have the dog tuned up and ready to go by opening day. The professional will have a colder eye than you and know exactly where the dog needs work and when it needs to be disciplined. But he should be careful about putting his dog with someone. Many so-called "trainers" are okay on retrievers but not so good with pointers, which take a lot more time and effort. Check out the trainer and avoid one who is training more than eight dogs.

Also, I would say that you should disregard the old notion that bringing a bird dog into the house softens him. Go ahead and make the dog a companion and it will probably perform better for you as it will be eager to please. A professional handler in the quail belt of Georgia and Florida often makes a house dog of the best dog in his string.

———•———

One thing I would be sure to tell my friend who is getting started— read up on the sport. Start a library.

The literature of upland bird shooting ranges wide: from a small number of books that can be called literature through a number that are something less than that but still valuable as pleasure reading, on to good competent technical works and into the deep thickets of metallurgy and gunsmithing.

Bird hunting, for some reason, has never been the contemplative pastime that trout fishing is. Trout fishermen have produced so many

good books that a lot of us came to the sport through the literature rather than the other way around. Bird hunters, on the other hand, seem to shoot birds first and then, when they have become passionate about the sport, go to the books to deepen their appreciation or, perhaps, merely to pass some time between the seasons.

If there is one book that to my mind captures the soul of the man who hunts birds it would be *The Hunting Sketches* by Ivan Turgenev. The book is a classic of literature and the hunting in it is incidental to Turgenev's much larger purposes, one of which included exposing Russian feudalism for what it was. But the hunting scenes are there and they are masterful and the book puts you in mind of some ineffable thing . . . a feeling for how far the purest and eternal portions of life are from politics and the life of the cities.

A book that does not succeed as great literature but that seems bound to endure among Americans who like the outdoors is *The Old Man and the Boy* by Robert Ruark. This book was first serialized in *Field & Stream* in the fifties and it had a legion of devoted followers. I remember talking to a man in Alabama one night and not being very surprised when he told me, "That book showed me how I was raised."

The book is not strictly about bird hunting but some of the best material in the book is about quail hunting and Ruark has the feeling of most long-time quail hunters down cold. There is a lot of charm in Ruark's book and it is a fine gift for a boy who is just getting started. Some of the old man's lectures on conservation and sportsmanship are even more pertinent today than when they were first published.

Havilah Babcock also wrote for the old *Field & Stream*. He too was a bird hunter who, because he had to have a job, was head of the English Department at the University of South Carolina for a number of years. He wrote about bird hunting with good, gentle humor and the stories, like "I Don't Want to Shoot an Elephant," put you in mind of a sporting Mark Twain or Ring Lardner. Babcock is especially good on the eccentricities of dogs. Somewhere, in one of his stories, he describes a dog that crosses a near frozen creek to retrieve two down birds. Once on the other side, the dog (a pointer, naturally) realizes that he will have to make two cold trips to get the birds back to his master or find a way to carry them both in its mouth on one trip, the way the calendar painters often show dogs retrieving but that most hunters have never seen. Babcock watches breathlessly, thinking that perhaps this time his own dog will perform the fabled double retrieve. The dog studies and thinks and finally solves the whole matter neatly by eating one of the birds. It is a story that any bird hunter will nod appreciatively over.

Gene Hill is the present-day Babcock. He writes a column for *Field & Stream* and his pieces have been collected in several volumes. Hill is especially rewarding in a time when so many of the people writing about sport have become near mechanics in their obsession with gear and technique. Hill continues to go for the soul of the sport and he is especially good on dogs.

One of the best practical books I have read on any kind of upland bird shooting is Frank Woolner's *Grouse and Grouse Hunting*. Woolner has a lot to tell the reader and he tells it efficiently and clearly. The history and the biology are here in digestible form and quantity and after you have read this book you feel like you at least know the bird that you hunt but seldom see.

Another good volume on grouse is Burton Spiller's *Grouse Feathers*. This is an affectionate look at the sport and one man's lifetime love affair with it.

At a more technical level, there is *The Double Shotgun* by Don Zutz. This is a complete history and a very good and thorough manual on how the double gun works and what to look for from one that you are considering buying.

Shotgunning by Bob Brister is a good companion when you are learning to shoot. All the fundamentals are here in easily managed form.

There are, of course, all sorts of other books. Nash Buckingham ought to be read by serious bird hunters. So should Charles Waterman. And there's a newcomer named Ron Rau. And there are others. The reading won't make you shoot better but it will make you think better about your shooting and give you some solace between seasons. And there is something to be said for that.

So, after I had advised my friend on dogs and guns and clothes and books, he would be on his own. I would wish him well and know that he was getting into something that, once it had him, would never let go.

15

Final Points

Reading about bird hunting is a poor substitute for actually going out and hunting. But some of us are so far gone we will take whatever we can get. I once asked a dog trainer of vast experience how to get my dog to trail grouse without crowding them. "Best way I know is to shoot about 300 grouse over her," he said. "That'll make a good hunter out of her every time."

Yes, and it wouldn't be bad for the man holding the gun, either. He didn't say it because he didn't have to. Anybody who hunts birds probably cannot get enough because the season is short and there is just nothing else like it. There is simply nothing else like hunting for birds behind a dog. You cannot explain it to people who have never done it, especially if they do not want to hear, which is so often the case. You cannot really explain it to people who *do* it. Bird hunters will talk about their sport with each other but not the way that trout fishermen do. When bird hunters talk, it is generally about the dogs and how well they are working. But it is hard to convey the success of a hunt except by numbers and numbers don't tell very much of the story. Coveys flushed and birds in the bag is certainly a measure of something and only a fool would say that those numbers don't count at all. But they tell a woefully incomplete story.

What, then, is the measure of a good day or a good season?

Hard to say. You need to have some shooting, which means you need to be in places where there are birds. This means you've done some work and scouted and that, at least regarding bird coverts, you know the country. You need to have some good dog work. A day of chasing your dog down, looking for him, yelling at him, and apologizing to your partner for him can make bird hunting into a sour ordeal. So you want your dog to perform and, if the dog does, that means that you've done your work there, too.

You'd like to kill a reasonable share of the birds you shoot at. This does not mean you have to kill every bird you see or that you have to break into triple figures every season on grouse or get a dozen doubles on the covey rise if you are hunting quail. But you are out there to kill birds and that is by definition serious business. If you can't do it competently then you haven't taken a serious piece of business seriously enough. So you want to shoot with some ability and, if you do, that shows that you have studied and practiced.

All this preparation pays off for only two months or so when the weather turns and harvest is in the air. In a way, you are harvesting the fruits of your own labor. There is ritual in it and there is a return according to the extent of your own work and preparation.

A good hunt should also include a small element of surprise. In grouse hunting you often come across the remains of an old farm and even the small family plot, with the stones still standing and tended. I found one once where the five austere slabs of granite were all carved with dates that fell within a day or two of each other. An entire family, cut down by some epidemic. It is the kind of thing, especially at a time when the seasons are changing and winter is coming on, to make you think hard.

Hunting quail I have come across the remains of old peckerwood sawmills, abandoned sharecropper homes, tobacco-drying sheds, and a derelict brick kiln. Things to remind you that time passes, things change, and nothing is as it was except the changing of the seasons which, at moments like that, you feel acutely.

Though it is entirely satisfying to hunt alone—especially if you are hunting with a dog and, therefore, are not *really* alone—most of the best days seem to involve a partner. A good partner is someone

you hunt comfortably with. He's somebody who either says nothing or all the right things about your dog, doesn't hog shots or shoot competitively, and has a sense of humor.

On a good hunt in grouse country, you find a few old wind-seeded apple trees or an abandoned orchard and you'll eat an apple or two—bruised and blemished but still tart and firm to your teeth.

You come home pleasantly tired, with the afternoon going quickly to evening and the chill coming over the land like a drape. You have birds to clean or hang and even after you've washed up, your hands have that dark rich smell about them. You build a fire, have a drink, and feel that one of your alloted days is passing but that you did well by it.

That's a good day.